LEVERAGING ON GOD'S advantage

SEYI OLADOSU

Leveraging on God's advantage

Copyright © 2022, Seyi Oladosu. All rights reserved.

The author has asserted his right to be identified as the author of this work in accordance with the Copyright, Designs, and Patents Act 1988.

No part of this publication may be reproduced, stored in a retrieval system, or transmitted, in any form or by any means, electronic, mechanical, photocopying, recording, or otherwise, without the prior permission of the author.

All scripture quotations, unless otherwise indicated, are taken from the Holy Bible, King James Version, Cambridge University Press, Oxford University Press, HarperCollins and the Queen's Printers.

Published in the United Kingdom by Seyi Oladosu Publishing

ISBN: 978-1-7392146-0-9

Acknowledgment

First and foremost, I want to give praise and all glory to God Almighty for shining His light into my life and making this book possible, not by power nor might but by the Spirit of the Lord.

For the beautiful built-to-last ministry orientation given to me from the outset, I want to thank my pastor and leader, Pastor JF Odesola, who sent me out on the first mission. You are very special and peculiar.

My thanks go to my revered mentor, teacher, and coach, Rev George Adegboye, for all the push and exposure. He showed me how to do ministry and not run services, learning at his feet the art of preaching, engagement, organisation, and an ever-increasing study of the word.

My sincere thanks also go to Apostle Lawrence Achudume for giving me that first preaching shot.

For all your beautiful efforts, warmth, and sacrifices in getting this manuscript out into what it is today—writing out, arranging, proofreading, and editing, my deep appreciation goes to Pastor Fatai Kasali and Pastor Felix Makanjuola Jnr. You're unique—helpers of destiny. Thanks for everything.

Special thanks and appreciation to my wife and children for helping to make things work out and become possible. Lots of love. You're the best winning team in the world.

Contents

CHAPTER 1
Accessing God's Power 9

CHAPTER 2
Activating Divine Empowerment 23

CHAPTER 3
Rivers of Living Water 41

CHAPTER 4
Direct Dial with God 53

CHAPTER 5
Baptism of the Holy Spirit 63

CHAPTER 6
Trusting God's Plan for Your Life 83

CHAPTER 7
Maximised Results Through Prayer 89

CHAPTER 8
Coming Out Stronger 97

Introduction

The light shine in darkness, and darkness cannot stop the light. God is the centrepiece of all mankind. Without Him, we are nothing. In Him we live and move and have our being. He is the Vine, and we are the branches. When we abide in Him, He abides in us because without Him, we can do nothing.

With God, all things are possible. He's limitless. He has everything, owns everything, all-powerful, all-knowing, and is an ever-present help in times of need.

He has never failed nor lost a battle. He is God all by Himself. The unchangeable changer who is greater than the greatest, better than the best, richer than the richest, older than the oldest, beautiful for all situations, dependable, and reliable forevermore.

The fact that God is in us settles it all so we can depend on Him for everything and drink from the river of living water. Therefore, living and thriving on these advantages as His delight, redeemed people of the Lord, sought-out, and a city not forsaken, makes you and me a marvel, wonder, sought-after, and extraordinary to our world.

Don't be a shark in an aquarium but a shark that inexhaustibly explores the entire ocean.

How precious are your thoughts towards me, oh Lord! How great are they in number! If I should count them, they're more in number than the sand, when I'm awake, I am still with you (Psalm 139:17-18).

CHAPTER 1

Accessing God's Power

The Scripture says in Acts 10:38: *"How God anointed Jesus of Nazareth with the Holy Ghost and with power: who went about doing good, and healing all that were oppressed of the devil; for God was with him".*

There is a reason God gives power to His people or empowers them. God will not just give you power or ability or put enablement in an area of your life just for you to be an individual. It is for a purpose and a reason. If Jesus Christ needed the power of God to function as a purpose-driven individual, a man of God, and as a human, why then would anyone think they don't need the perpetual power of God in their lives?

How God anointed Jesus of Nazareth with the Holy Ghost and with power... "And what did He do with the power? He *"went about doing good, and healing all that were oppressed of the devil; for God was with him* (Acts 10:38).

After God empowers us, He still goes with us to ensure that the power is appropriately used in the right direction and in the right sense. God makes sure it works in the direction He intends. Let's consider the man in the Book of John chapter five, the man by the pool of Bethesda. This man stayed by the Bethesda pool because something was seriously wrong with his life. He was in a situation where nothing was progressing for thirty-eight years, which is more than half of the lifespan of a man. However, things changed the day Jesus came to that place by the pool of Bethesda. You may spend half of your life crippled, perhaps spiritually or physically, or in certain areas, but do you know you need God's strength—the power of God? This man needed the power of God in his life, having stayed in this same spot for thirty-eight years. If you have been in the same spot for years as an individual or a church, you don't need a rocket scientist to inform you again that you need God's power in your life.

For thirty-eight years, this man was in the same spot. He couldn't progress; he couldn't go forward and was just there, rolling in and out. Nothing happened in his life. His purpose failed, his dreams were not coming to pass, his life was empty, and God's purpose for his life was stagnant. He was not accomplishing anything. Perhaps you have come to that spot in your life and wondered that you're still in the same place despite trying everything. That man was in the same spot, and then Jesus Christ showed up. The Scripture says, *"How God anointed Jesus of Nazareth with the Holy Ghost and with power: who went about doing good."* He wasn't going to and fro. A person who goes to and fro seeks people's destruction—to kill, steal, and destroy. What's the name of the person who fits this description? Satan.

However, Jesus Christ was going with purpose. He was a purpose driven human being who has been loaded with God-enabling power for a reason, to fulfil His destiny and God's purpose. Now, may I ask you this day, every power God has given you, what have you done with it? So many people cry and say God give me power, but God keeps saying, *What have you done with the one I gave you? What have you done with the character-moulding power I gave you? What have you achieved with that encouraging power I gave you? What about the power to get wealth that I gave you? That innovative-creative power I gave you, that power to love I gave you, that large heart I gave you? What have you done with it? What have you done with the power to transform minimum into maximum?*

God is saying, *what have you done with that power?* Until Jesus Christ came to the pool on this day, nothing happened in this man's life. Does it mean he had nothing in him to trigger God's power? He had, but guess what? He was weak and had no might again. Many people have no reason to live again, even though they exist. They have lost touch with the world, and they have lost touch with God. They still exist; they are not living for dreams again—no aspiration. They've got and developed a flat tyre and knocked-out engine but still coasting. Introspect yourself, are you just coasting?

Have you ever seen a car coasting down the hill? You don't need to apply pressure or any energy to accelerate. Are you just going on free lands this day without God's power for purpose in your life? Jesus Christ, the anointed of God and the Holy Spirit, went about doing good, healing those who were oppressed of the devil because God was with Him. This same Jesus came to the pool of Bethesda, the pool with five porches, where all the sick and derelicts were.

I want you to stretch your imagination a bit. Do you know the area could be smelling, but Jesus didn't care? He went there anyway because He had God's power and purpose in His life to function. So, by the time He got there, He did not wait for this man's excuse. My prayer for you today is that God will bypass all your excuses in the name of Jesus Christ. He will look beyond them and reach out to you. God keeps saying I have given you the power and empowerment that comes from above to change position. This man desired to move from point A to B, but God had a better plan for him because God wanted him to move to point Z. Hence, God bypassed all his excuses immediately and said, *Rise up, take your bed and walk.*

Jesus did not hesitate to shake up the man's world. The power was already there; Jesus Christ needed to make contact with it. Remember, the Scripture says, *"and you shall receive power after the Holy Ghost has come upon you"*. The Holy Ghost came upon you on the day of your salvation. There is a difference between the indwelling and the filling of the Holy Spirit. When you gave your life to Jesus Christ, the Holy Spirit came to dwell in you, so you have received power the day you were baptized in the Holy Spirit. Guess what happens? He came to fill you, that is why it is in constant measure.

Hence, you need to hunger for more measures of the Holy Spirit every time. Cry out to Him and say: *Holy Spirit, fill me again. Baptize me again.* Every time you have communion, wake up, or are at a crossroads, cry out and say: *Holy Spirit, fill me again.* This prayer is different from the Spirit dwelling in you. The Holy Spirit is already dwelling in you, and that is the embodiment of God's power.

And you shall receive power after the Holy Ghost has come upon you and you shall be God's witnesses in Jerusalem, Samaria, in Judea and the uttermost part of the earth (Acts 1:8).

That power of influence God gave you, what are you doing with it? What about the power to turn dreams into great things? What are you doing with it? Jesus Christ went about doing good, healing all those oppressed of the devil. Do you know what most are doing with the power today in the Body of Christ? We are using it to eat Chinese rice, spare ribs, and burgers with the kings inside.

Even to pray now is trouble, and seeking your dreams' fulfilment has become mountainous, surmounting problems around you. You don't even know how to balance the equation again. Every day you wake up in uncertainty, God is upset with you because there is a power in you meant to be used. Every day, you are to activate the power of the Holy Spirit to come upon and work for you, bringing joy and encouragement to every situation you find yourself.

My question for you this day is, how much good are you worth? How good are you? How much good are you doing right now? What are you doing with what God has given you in your life? What have you done with all the talents, gifts, character, and possession God has given you? We have had cases of kings in the Bible who have used their position to bring idolatry and evil to destroy people. What are you doing with your possession in the Body of Christ, neighbourhood, family, community, and everywhere you find yourself? Are you an uprooter? Are you a destroyer or God's planter? Are you God's harvester and somebody God can rely upon on this earth? Can God rely on you in the neighbourhood where you live, where you work, and in your family? Can God depend on you because His power is in your life?

I will share with you **six power packs** around understanding how the power of God works. These are the six things you need to know:

1. We need to understand that the benefit of God's power has already been made available to us.

Not only has His power been made available to us, but so have His benefits in every aspect of our lives if we will accept them. You can't be sick, and you have the power of God working in your life. When God says I have given you the power to lay hands on the sick for them to recover, including yourself at that point in time, what do you do? You lay hands if you are sick, afflicted, or have pain in your body. Lay hands on yourself, and then let the power be triggered to function. Seize it as an opportunity and take advantage of God's ability. You can't just begin to look around you and see things not working, folding your hands, and just watching. In the Book of Nehemiah chapter one and chapter two, Nehemiah's countenance changed after they told him that the wall of Jerusalem had been destroyed and people had gone to prison. He said things had to be done, even as he stood before the king. The king, Artaxerxes, asked him why he was sad. You can read the entire chapter one and two. Nehemiah said his people had been enslaved, the city walls of his country had broken down, and things were not working the way God wanted them to.

Now, there is a new vision growing in Nehemiah that is bringing righteous indignation. There is something about righteous indignation and ordinary indignation. A righteous indignation is what will make Elijah tear down the prophets of Baal's temple and Asherah. There is righteous indignation when we reject idolatry and unrighteousness in all forms. In this instance, a wave of anger will erupt in you when you see walls meant to lift people up broken down. A righteous indignation comes from you when you see Satan oppressing and attacking God's people, and you just cannot fold your hands and say *it is well*. I don't know where they got the 'it is well' from, like they say in churches nowadays. They don't even know what they are talking about. Instead of saying *come on, something has to be done. We are chasing the devil out of your house, business, body, and finances, in the name of Jesus.* If two of us shall agree on earth as touching an issue, it shall be done for us by our Father who is in Heaven. We must be bold to command it out in the name of Jesus Christ. We must command Satan to lose his grip and hold.

Instead, what do they say? *It is well,* and they look at you suspiciously. It's time to command power. Power must change hands; power must be accessed. Power must be combined and unified to chase out the devil. Couples must join hands to chase out the devil. People of God must join hands together to chase out the devil. Our family must join hands to chase out the devil from their vicinity and territory because power is available for us. Seize and take advantage of it.

2. The power of God has been packaged in several ways to make it available to us.

How will I get this power? God has packaged it in several ways, which is why you have Christian books, literature, the word of God, CDs, DVDs, and television broadcasts of good ministries everywhere. You can access and acquire them, but what are you doing? We are not seizing it. For instance, how many copies of your church's CD/DVD messages are in your house? Can we find three in ten? Why? Because some feel it is not compulsory and there is no need for it. There is a need for it because this is how God packaged His power and made it available for you and me every day of our lives. We should not be without the power of God 24/7. There should be something going in your ears every time.

Faith comes by hearing and hearing by the word of God. A word of purpose should come out of your mouth every time. For with our mouth, we shall be justified or condemned. The word of your mouth saves you, and whatsoever I say with my mouth, I believe and receive it by heart. By heart, we believe unto righteousness, and by mouth, confession is made unto salvation. Something must come out of your mouth and go into you to build your faith and life. That is how to activate God's power in you. You can't just exist every day with this carefree attitude that many people have in the Body of Christ towards the power of God. Demons are now standing instead of trembling where you are. Demons should be trembling where you are. They shouldn't find it comfortable and standing easy where you are. They should run as soon as they see you. They shouldn't stay around you.

Have you ever seen a housefly perch upon a hot iron? Where would the flies go when you put two kinds of iron together, a cold one and a hot iron, and allow flies to perch on them? Of course, it is on the cold iron. Would any fly settle on the hot iron? NO. Some Christians are already cold and flat, so you see 'flies' perching all around them. You must be determined to increase and raise the temperature around you everywhere. Don't let demons have the opportunity to stay all around you. Don't let evil forces be able to hold their plans all around you. If you need to bind them or release fire to burn them, do it irrespective of what they are or who they are.

3. Various packages that make His power available to us are transferable, contagious, and transmittable.

The power of God can come into your life in various ways, means, and packages, and they are mobile. They are communicable and transmissible. Whenever you hear the word of God, the power of God is being transmitted, but guess what? You can start thinking of chicken and chips, getting nothing there. However, when your mind is right with God, and you open your heart and say *I am just going to receive it at all cost and by all means*, it shows you are hungry. You are picked and next in line if you are ready to receive the power of God and prepared to receive the activation.

Laying on of hands can transfer the power of God. In some churches, some people don't come to church any time there is a laying on of hands. They miss it. Some people don't come to church whenever there is a communion service. They think having communion is like the Anglican, Methodist, and African Church, where you should not go to church if you are in a position of sin. Instead of seeing the house of God as a house of prayer and a solution centre whereby you receive God's grace and new strength to forsake and never go back to it, many people see it as a time to reject communion. Some will say, *my heart is not right;*

the Bible already says if I eat it unworthily, I will die. The shocking thing is you will die one day if you keep running away from it like that and standing unworthily away from God. How long will you run unworthily away from God, your Father?

In Luke chapter 15, the prodigal son said *in my father's house, is there no better food? Here, I am eating pigs' food and all these things that pigs eat. I will arise and go to my father, and I will say, Father, forgive me; I am not worthy of being called your son again.*

Now, instead of emulating the above, most Christians run away from God. The more you preach about holiness, the more you see people run away from the Church. God is a solution to every predicament. People should run more to God and not run away when they commit sexual sins and all kinds of illegalities and unrighteousness.

4. God gives His power to us for every situation.

If you need power for wealth, to live holy, to succeed, or to come out of obscurity, God can provide it irrespective of what the enemy thinks about you and me.

Arnold Schwarzenegger, a man from Austria, who went to America with just a nylon bag, one pair of trousers and one shirt as an illegal immigrant, one day discovered he had a great body. Later, he went into body building. He built his body until he saw a competition in some places and enrolled. He won and still kept building his body until one day, some movie producers saw him on television and decided to search for him, casting him as a movie star. He agreed, even with his inability to speak good English. For somebody reading this, God has given you a great body, talent, beauty, brain, and hand. He has made you smart, but look at you right now; what have you done with it?

I don't know what the Church is turning into with this *'grab it, take it, receive it, it's yours'* mantra, which some people think is how God works, like magic. No! God had to use what He had given you. He has given you brain, arms, feet, beauty, skills, talents, opportunity, and voice. Arnold Schwarzenegger did the first movie to the sixth movie. Now look at Arnold, the illegal immigrant living in a mansion and enjoying a life of splendour. Look at all the movies he acted in and how great he was.

Then, suddenly, he woke up one day and desired to be a politician. Knowing they don't allow illegal immigrants to contest for anything in America, he went to join the Republican party. He influenced them from the grassroots to change the law to favour illegal immigrants. They started passing the bill. He failed repeatedly until one day, they incorporated into the bill the fact that immigrants could run for public office in America except for the presidency. The next thing before then is that he went to marry a Kennedy. You can't marry a Kennedy and not be influential in America. The Kennedys are top shots in America. So, he married Maria Shriver, and God blessed their marriage. They went forward, and so one day, he declared his interest in the seat of the Governor of California. Let's consider where he came from: a nylon bag, one pair of trousers, one shirt, and bodybuilding.

The question is, are you using what God has given you right now? What are you doing with it? Peter Mandelson is now Lord Mandelson. Some thirty years ago in the university, he took a few undergraduates together and said, *common guys, we are nobody today as undergraduates, but we can turn the history of Great Britain in the next thirty years. We can do it. This is what we are going to do: here, you criticise gays and homosexuals, saying we don't know why they must allow them.*

Within thirty years, he took all the other people, sat down together, joined their hands, burned the midnight oil, and said, *we are going to change this country.* The first thing we know is that Tony Blair came to power. Half of them came into the government, and half came later. Soon, they started influencing the laws of the land.

Sexual orientation laws: they are the ones behind it. No, you should not be running from them but rather leading them to Christ and letting them know the path of life. We must show them that this is a reprobate mind and God doesn't want you to take the form of godliness but deny the power thereof. That is not how God works. God didn't make you a woman; you are a man! You don't have to do a sex change to become somebody in this world we live in.

Do you think it was somebody who just woke up one day and bam, the change happened? No, for thirty years, they have been planning this. Here you are, you and I, even to pray is trouble for you. You find it hard to sing and worship. To declare the word of God and carry your Bible openly on the street is trouble for you. Is it easy come and easy go? No, God doesn't work like that. You have to give God something to work with to make you great.

I pray for you today; your name shall be great. Arnold Schwarzenegger was the governor of California, the fifth largest economy in the whole world. He came with one pair of trousers and one rumpled shirt inside one nylon bag as an illegal immigrant who didn't know where his next meal would come from. Now, he has influenced more on the laws in America. I have seen people like Barak Obama becoming president, and next election, you will see people like Arnold Schwarzenegger contesting for the presidency in America. Despite this, some will say *I am just an oversea student. I am just here to study* like some parents did when they came from an African country to the UK to study. These parents took all their children and went back home. Children have to come back again and start begging for a British passport which was already their entitlement in the first place, because of the self centred attitude and parochialism of parents who came to the UK and didn't see any opportunity.

I don't know whether you are like Arnold Schwarzenegger or not. You may be somebody who is daydreaming and not experiencing or expecting anything—just waking up to ordinary life. One year you have been in a different country, two, three years, even up to nine years; what have you done? What have you accomplished? The opportunity may not last long if you don't seize the moment. It may be a door is about to close; you can never tell. Therefore, seize the opportunity you have right now. Some of you have been given the power to rebrand something—companies, logos, names, corporations, and so on. You have a good ability to do public relations and merchandise things. Some people are fashion designers, really creative, and can do things, but they fall short every time.

Many people are still bound by the spirit of fear—the fear of heights, fear of tomorrow, fear of money, fear of succeeding, fear of getting married, fear of driving, fear of doing this or that, and even fear of having a driver's license. Go and get your license. You can't fail; if you fail once, do it again. People like Michael Faraday, who discovered electricity, Albert Einstein, and Bill Gates, repeatedly failed until they succeeded. Richard Branson, in his book, said *Screw it, Let's do it*. Whenever he thinks about this statement, *let's do it whether or not we fail. If we fail, we fail*; he succeeds every time he reads this. The day he came out to form Virgin Atlantic to compete against the almighty British Airways, they said he would fail. His profit went up, and because everybody saw British Airways as too expensive with no one offering a competitive price at a good deal, people decided to go for it. British Airways got angry; they brought all kinds of campaigns against him, including lawsuits.

Nevertheless, Richard Branson kept on climbing the mountain. He kept on doing it. The next thing he was doing was Virgin music. He was buying all the record shops in the country then, and here you are, sitting down. Some people think of something different inside the church when message is going on instead of saying, *Holy Spirit, connect me! Where do I find myself here?*

5. Jesus operated by the power of God He accessed.

You may have the power of God, but if you don't access it, it won't work. You may have a computer, but you will never use it if you don't turn it on and put in your password. It's not yours until your password is on the computer, and then the operating system comes up. You can carry your laptop from now till tomorrow and put it on your shoulder or armpit, showing the whole world you have a laptop. Even children have laptops today, but a laptop you don't use won't give you access. In a nutshell, the powers you don't utilise, you won't access! Until Jesus Christ accessed the power of God, He could not do anything. He could not heal those that were oppressed of the devil. God could not prove His presence in His life, but immediately He accessed God's power, He just came to those distressed and said, *Satan, loose him and let him go*. He went somewhere again and said, *"Woman, thou art loose"*. What was He doing? He was accessing the power. But here you are, carrying God's power all about, saying, *I have got the power*, but you need to start using it. You need to access and utilise it.

In the case of Jairus' daughter in the Bible, Jesus said go ahead; we are coming. He got there and said *Talitha Cumi*. What was He doing? He was accessing the power, utilising it, and releasing it. *Talitha cumi*, which means *little girl, arise*. That is it! A deaf and dumb man came, and He looked at him, and He said, *Ephphatha*, meaning *be opened*, and his ears and speech were restored. What was He doing? He was accessing the power of God and utilising it. You can't just be a Christian, and everybody is laughing at you in your office. They don't even know whether you are born again or not. They are swearing around you, and you are laughing. You said as long as I didn't smile or talk with them, but that is foolishness. You need to let them know you are a child of God and that you carry power.

A man told me some time ago that he had back pain and had been to the hospital. I said *come to our church, we will anoint you, and you will be healed completely.* As a matter of fact, if our landlord said *look, I have this problem.* I will say *come to our church.* If these hospitals can't help you, my God will do it. The landlord might even say the next one-year rent, take it free of charge, afterward, who knows.

6. We can access the power of God through:

The Holy Spirit

The blood of Jesus

The name of Jesus

The word of God

With the Holy Spirit, the Blood of Jesus, the Name of Jesus, and the word of God, no Devil can bug you again. No situation can stand against you, and no ugly situation can arise itself and gain the upper hand in your life again, in the name of Jesus.

CHAPTER 2

Activating Divine Empowerment

Behold, I give you the authority to trample on serpents and scorpions, and over all the power of the enemy, and nothing shall by any means hurt you. **LUKE 10:19**

Your physical existence is forgotten, and your spiritual existence now takes over. Life continues from this physical world into a new realm where you operate on a higher frequency with God; that is where eternity comes in. Why we do not look at the things which are seen, for the things which are seen are temporary, but we look at things which we do not see, for the things which we do not see are eternal. So, for most of us, when the wind comes, we forget all the faith words we've deposited in our minds that we are the head and not the tail. We forget we can do all things through Christ, who gives us strength despite the wind blowing and waves raging everywhere. It is like being in a boat rocking side to side, but you're holding on, crying out: *somebody, help me! Who will help me here now!?* You have suddenly left God's confinement, which empowers you to overcome that storm. Instead of you confessing that *I am an overcomer, I am more than a conqueror through Him that loves me*, you are here, screaming and saying, *I am going to die!*

This wave will submerge this boat and then sink, and that will be the end of it.

Alternatively, say, *I know my redeemer liveth. I know I will get to the end of the journey and get through this trouble. I know it's not going to kill or submerge me.* Guess what? God comes to empower you. When you know what you are going through right now is temporary, knowing our God will get the glory at the end of it all, that is when God now comes to empower you. When you say I know I may not have enough money today to get this job done, but it's sure *"my God shall supply all of my needs according to His riches in glory by Christ Jesus"*, God begins to empower and strengthen you.

Because of our experience with Christ and our relationship with God, some things are made available to us automatically. When I was born into my father's house, I automatically became a bearer of his name. Everything he had, I have a link to claim by inheritance. As a result of being born into my father's family, some things were laid into a precedence to become mine as a descendant of that family. When we become born again, God automatically guarantees some things to happen and work for us. He positions us in areas of blessing, empowerment, and miracle.

For example, Prophet Isaiah said, *"But they that wait upon the Lord shall renew their strength"*. God also said, *"They that wait upon the Lord shall not be ashamed"*. The Bible also said, *"I am the Lord that heal you"*; *"I will not put these diseases of Egypt upon you"*. God spoke all these words; He said by my stripes, you are healed. Because of being born again and belonging to God's family, some things were put in place as a blessing for you to walk in. God put many things in store for all, making us understand that our experiences and relationship with God are not ordinary. Receiving Christ into your life entitles you to some things. And when this happens, we step into an opportunity called Positional Truth: *"my*

God shall supply all of my needs according to His riches in glory by Christ Jesus". Is that true or not? By your position in Christ, this becomes yours. But it doesn't necessarily get manifested until you begin to make it work, isn't it? When God says *"you are the head and not the tail"*, is that what He says or not? That is what He says about you. But how will it happen in your life? Will you just hold the Bible and say *look at it, now it is in the Bible: "I am the head and not the tail"*? Yet, everybody slaps you around everywhere. How will that positional truth now be manifested? That is what I want to talk about here.

God has given all of us power. He said, *"I am the Lord that heals you"*, yet we still live with sicknesses, diseases, pains, and discomfort. We know this is a positional truth. However, by our position and righteousness in Christ, some things are automatically put in place for us. For example, when you work for a company, you are automatically qualified to receive a pension and benefits from that company. When you are born again, you automatically have a portion of the Lord's blessing, but we are saying these blessings may never come to fruition in our lives without them being activated. You can't just have it in the Bible, and then it is not happening in your life, despite knowing it's yours.

For example, you have an account with Barclays Bank, and they gave you a bank card and a PIN because you now belong to a family of Barclays since you are a customer. If you are not a customer of Barclays, you don't have access to the card's benefits and PIN. So now, what does the PIN do for you? The PIN helps you activate your account, and every time you slot it into the machine in the wall or anywhere you want to use your account, you have to access it with a PIN. Accessing that account is what we call today 'activating the account'. God has opened an account for you called the account of blessing by virtue of you being born again. But those blessings cannot be manifested until you activate them.

Many of us born-again and Holy Spirit-filled believers have been given the promises of the Lord, but these promises are not operating in our lives because we have not moved from the Positional Truth into the next stage called Progressional Truth. When God says we are healed by the stripes of Jesus Christ, and I have sickness, affliction, and even pain in my body, what I need to do is to go on and access the positional truth. The positional truth is sitting down and waiting for me to do something and make a move. It is waiting right there, just like Jesus Christ standing by you and the devil also standing by you. The devil is attacking you, Jesus Christ is doing nothing, and you wonder why the Lord is not intervening. *Didn't He see that the devil was attacking me? Look at what the devil is doing to me. Why is Jesus not doing anything?* But Jesus Christ keeps waiting, and suddenly, you look at Jesus and say, *You are my righteousness; you are my peace; you are my deliverer; you are my hope. You are the glory and the lifter up of my head. I am more than a conqueror through Him that loved me.* Then you begin to declare: "*No weapon formed against me shall prosper, every tongue that speak against me in judgement I condemn*", and then you begin to look at Satan and say, *I have submitted myself to God, and I resist you in the name of Jesus.*

The Bible says that when you resist, he flees from you, and then you'll begin to see Satan fleeing away. Who activated that power? Was it Christ or you? It's you, of course. You will activate it, and then He will make it work. He has done His job by bringing you into this family and opening the book of blessings for you, but it won't be manifested until you activate the power to make it a reality. It's not just about carrying the Bible and saying *I am born again* or *a Christian*. There must be fruit in your life; there must be works operating in your life. There must be activation of God's power in our lives, or else, the world will ask us and say, *I thought you said you are a Christian, why is your life not better? Why are you still sick? Why are you still broke? Why are you still living in sin and unrighteousness? Why does satanic power still bind you? Why are demons still molesting and demoralising you? What is going on? I thought you said you were born again?* How can you be born again and demons will be pressing you down on the bed when Jesus Christ said, *I have given you authority over all unclean spirits?*

How can a demon be having sex with you on your bed in your own house, and you are born again? When Jesus Christ says, *"I have given you power to trample on snakes and scorpions and over all the power of the enemy, and nothing shall by any means hurt you"*, it is not just written there for fancy. It is for you to possess it, and I want to tell you it has to start from somewhere. Look at these first scriptures we will consider:

"Behold, I give unto you power to tread on serpents and scorpions, and over all the power of the enemy: and nothing shall by any means hurt you" (Luke 10:19).

What is a serpent? Satan! So, if a snake has been working or walking in you, through body movement, in your belly, over your feet, or something all around you, today, God says you should trample on it. He says your body is the temple of the Holy Spirit, so command it to come out in the name of Jesus. That is what God said you should do there: was I the one who said you should do that? It is God. What are the scorpions mentioned in the verse above? Satanic agents that bring discomfort and pain or affliction. The pains will just come with its stings, and it stings you like that and then goes back again. That is how the devil breaks your focus. When the devil wants to break your focus, you know what he does? Have you seen a cobra snake before? It is usually black and has a flat head. Any time it wants to attack, it fixes its gaze on the prey, flattens its head, and mesmerises the victim, which people call hypnotisation in the world here in alternative medicine. It hypnotises you to break your focus and empowerment to destroy him, and when he is doing that, he's putting fear in your heart, but 2 Timothy 1:7 says:

"For God hath not given us the spirit of fear; but of power, and of love, and of a sound mind."

As you continue to declare the scripture above, also say *I rebuke you in the name of Jesus* because the plan is to try and break your focus. He is trying to suck your spiritual energy level out of you so you will be empty. He wants to inject foolishness into you, and if that happens, fear begins to take over your life, and then he strikes.

The same goes for the scorpion; there is something it's got on its back called the sting (very poisonous stings). When it wants to strike, it carries it up, looks for the victim, and punctures, then deposits the poison. The effect of that poison can be crippling and brutal. People can die from scorpion stings. In the same way, Satan comes in the power of that scorpion with its poison. He looks around for his victim, and when he sees a believer lazing around, careless, with a bad attitude, he strikes and punctures a hole, depositing the poison. The scripture we read in Luke 10:19 says,

"Behold, I give unto you power to tread on serpents and scorpions and over all the power of the enemy..."

All the enemy's power to discourage you, mess you up, molest you, mesmerise you, and make you feel like nothing will come to nought because God said He had given you power over all the power of the enemy. Anything the enemy can do to cut your life short and prevent you from enjoying the Lord's blessings, whatever it is, God said I had given you power over that power of the enemy, and nothing shall by any means hurt you. Is there anything hurting you today? Anything hurting you today in your spirit, soul, and body, God has given you the authority to trample them all: *nothing shall by any means hurt you!* This is how God empowers you to break every power and dominion of the evil ones.

"But thou shalt remember the LORD thy God: for it is he that giveth thee power to get wealth, that he may establish his covenant which he sware unto thy fathers, as it is this day" (Deuteronomy 8:18).

This is another level of power that God has given to you and me. The first one is the power to trample upon snakes and scorpions, and over every power of the enemy. Therefore, all power of the enemy is under you—the power of poverty is also under you. God has given you another power to get wealth, and it didn't say God will give you wealth. God's plan is to prosper us,

"I wish above all things that thou mayest prosper and be in health, even as thy soul prospereth" (3 John 2).

So, what did He do further, as He empowers you to get wealth? You now receive wisdom. Somebody like Bill Gates received wisdom to get wealth: just to manufacture software with a mind that says, *I want to see a computer on every desk worldwide. I want to see computers in every office and home worldwide*, and that's it. That was what drove him to become crazy and started manufacturing software, and every computer now has Microsoft on it.

Another example is the man who invented Coca-Cola many years ago. One man mixed all the things and said this is nice. This is a substitute for water, and I think it will sell. Then he invented CocaCola and kept it because he didn't know what to do with it. Later, another man heard that this man invented Coca-Cola, and he had a new vision, and the vision was if I could lay my hand on that Coca-Cola, I would bring it, mix it in water, and put it in many containers. Do you remember the story in 2 Kings, chapter 4? According to the word of prophet Elisha, the woman with the pot of oil kept pouring the oil until there was no more vessel.

See? This is where all these principles came from. It's we Christians who are not tapping into it and understanding it. The principle of Coca-Cola came from 2 Kings chapter 4, pouring oil into vessels.

This man said if I could get that mixture the man made, I would mix it and pour it into many bottles. It was bottles everywhere; they never invented cans in those days. He said I would just take it to all those shops, everywhere in this state, and then I see it going all over the United States. So, he went to the man and approached him tactfully. Unfortunately, some of us lack tactics and good attitudes as Christians. The way we approach people, even on the phone, is cold. For example, your phone rings now, and the next thing you say is *hello, who is this?* It may be someone who wants to bless your life. Some of you have been praying to God for help, but look at your approach and attitude: *who is this? Yes, wrong number.* And the person says, *Is that Mr so and so*, and you say, *yes, and so what?* Do you see our attitude?

Now, some of us work in an office, and instead of saying: *Hello! Good afternoon, this is so and so. How may I help you?* You say *who are you? Who is speaking? Who is on the line?* And so on. They just put the phone down, but you don't know who is on the other side of the line. You don't know if it is the president of a country. You don't know if it's the CEO of a corporation you want to do business with or start a career. It may be they see your CV and are calling you up, but see your attitude? Just look at the approach of this man without anything in his hand. He said *excuse me, Mr A, you have invented this Coca-Cola. I think it's very good and I want to buy from you at any price. Name your price.* Eyes on greed; no vision: any time a person lacks vision, their eyes will pop out in greed. The greed of let me just get it now. Some are dating somebody but can't wait. All they want to do is to have sex with the person and say they just need to test each other and see. They say they want to know whether or not you are a virgin. Don't be a fool; no, you don't have to do that stupid thing. It is mundane.

Greed won't let you see the future or a better tomorrow. Greed will only let you see today, but guess what? My greatness is in my tomorrow. When tomorrow comes, tomorrow is the day that I wish for today. When tomorrow comes today, it became yesterday, and so I step into my tomorrow with a new vision. *"Blessed be the Lord, who daily load us with benefit, even the God of our salvation"* (Psalm 68:19). Every portion of benefit for each day of your life, you will not miss it in Jesus' name.

So, when the man about the Cola-Cola story told the fellow his intention, he said, *wait a minute, you want to buy this whole thing that I have spent all my life mixing and then coming up to this point, and you want me to name the price? Bring five hundred dollars.* Then the other man said, *give me a moment. I will be right back*, and he brought five hundred dollars, gave it to the inventor, and took the patent. You know how Jacob stole the birthright of Esau, remember? Don't let anybody steal your birthright. You have it; it's a big price for you. Don't let people steal it. He gave him five hundred dollars and took the entire patent, the whole thing he had been mixing all his life. He forfeited it for five hundred dollars because of lack of vision, and this man took it, established a mixing room in his kitchen, and started mixing this thing. He started corking this thing and sending it out. After realising that demands were coming, he started making more. Today, that five hundred dollars became fifty billion dollars that he bought from that man, and up till now, nobody knows the secret of Coca-Cola. Even those who work there just know they get some things from its delivery and by its package and then mix it somewhere, and that's it. What are we talking about here? There is empowerment to get wealth.

Another example is about a couple in this country [UK]. They came here from abroad to look for a job but couldn't get one. They were offered a cleaning job and security, and they said no.

They offered the woman a job to wash corpses, and she said no. She said *I know what I am built for. My husband won't do security.*

One day, they said, *look, I thought we loved this plantain thing. Let's slice this plantain, fry it, and then give it to that shop; maybe they would buy it.* So they turned their kitchen around and started slicing plantain. They started cutting and frying it and then sent it to the shop. And what happened next? The shop said, *bring more*, and before you know it, from morning till evening, they were frying plantain. They have to bring more relatives to come and help them join and fry plantain. They sent it to this park shop, Asian shops, and all the shops in their community.

They went beyond that to another borough. They kept spreading to another until one day, somebody came and said this thing you are selling, we like it spicy. Put some pepper inside. So, they experimented, put some, added spices in some, and then sent it. The spicy one moved more than ever, so they said this was good. This is what we should have been doing all this while, and we are wasting our lives looking for a job, sending CVs everywhere. Until now, they don't know what their CVs look like again. But what are they selling? Plantain chips, some spicy and some with honey. Have you seen Walkers crisp before? Now they are packaging it like Walkers crisp, and they are Nigerians.

Have you heard of the man who was selling groundnuts? He has bought two jets. He is in America, but here you are. God said in 3 John 3: *"Beloved, I wish above all things that thou mayest prosper and be in health, even as thy soul prospereth"*.

And in Deuteronomy 8:18, the Scripture says, *"But thou shalt remember the LORD thy God: for [it is] he that giveth thee power to get wealth, that he may establish his covenant which he sware unto thy fathers, as [it is] this day"*.

And here you are, looking for one dumb job, and they keep turning you back, and you keep saying maybe you should try something else. Try it first; people that try and fail keep trying until they become successful. Today's light bulb was done by a man who kept trying one thousand times. He tried and failed until he made it after one thousand times. Bill Gates failed with nobody to encourage or help him, but one day, somebody believed and gave him a hundred dollars, and he achieved a whole empire today! Look at Deuteronomy 8:18 again.

It is a covenant, isn't it? Now quickly go to Psalm 89:34, which says, *"My covenant will I not break, nor alter the thing that is gone out of my lips."*

God is not a man, that he should lie; neither the son of man, that he should repent: hath he said, and shall he not do it? or hath he spoken, and shall he not make it good? (Numbers 23:19).

Look at Hebrews 6:18: *"That by two immutable things, in which it was impossible for God to lie, we might have a strong consolation, who have fled for refuge to lay hold upon the hope set before us".*

This is where God empowers us, and we have become blind to our own needs, greed, and temporary things. All we care about is getting this bill paid, but we are not planning to be a blessing.

Look at another scripture here: *"He giveth power to the faint; and to [them that have] no might he increaseth strength"* (Isaiah 40:29).

Let the weak say I am strong; let the poor say I am rich. Whether you are weak in your body, emotions, marriage, finances, attitude, or interhuman relationships, God says He will give you strength. *"He gives power to the faint and those that have no might......"*. Stop saying, are you sure I can do my own business? Are you sure I can become that person God says? Are you sure I am more than a conqueror? Are you sure I am blessed and favoured? Are you sure God's favour is around me? Are you sure God's blessing is upon me? Are you sure I am the head and not the tail? Is it that you have no might to believe? Just know for sure that God will increase your strength.

God called Gideon a mighty man of valour. In my own words, Gideon said, *who is your mighty man of valour? Forget it; I am not your mighty man of valour. I am just minding my own business beating this wheat that I may make it to wine. This is what we do here.* Then the Angel of God said *mighty man of valour.* He did not recognise what God put on the inside of him. He saw himself as a weakling, as a person of low might, but it took God to open his eyes to convince him and say: *you are a mighty man of valour*, and I am going to prove it to you in a moment by bringing out a troop. You are the one going to deliver my people from the Midianites. Midianites people are wicked people. They are people who put you in a container, and your thinking becomes small. They mess up everything around you and never allow you to see your future. They are the people who kill your vision. Midianites people are containerised people. They contain you on the spot; they are small talkers and thinkers. They don't see the view of anything, and this why they are wicked people.

So he said, you will deliver My people from the Midianites, mighty man of valour. Then Gideon replied that if he truly was a mighty man of valour, the angel should make this cotton wool wet. That is easy for God. So, God brought dew from heaven, and the cotton wool became wet. He then said let it dry up if truly I am a mighty man of valour. God brought wind and then dried the cotton wool up.

Have some things ever happened to you, and you became scared? You thought you couldn't get it. You thought you couldn't become it. You thought it couldn't happen for you, and you are the least likely to succeed, maybe in your family, church, office, and everywhere. People just look at you small, and they say that guy from Africa or wherever you came from, forget him. Forget that woman or lady. But suddenly, the hands of the clock come, and it was you they pick, and you say, *are you sure of this?* That is how God arranges it. He said He gives power to the faint and those who have no might, He increased their strength. Suddenly, your influence increases.

There is a pastor from Nigeria who came to live in England, and after just a few years, he possessed what people who have been living in this country right from birth never had. Suddenly, the queen called him one day and said we have heard of what you have been doing in your borough, helping to see the gun and knife crimes go down, working with the police. So, on this date, I am going to give you MBE. This is a young man from Nigeria, and he got an MBE. Politicians don't have MBE; people in the house of lords don't have MBE, and there are categories of people that have MBE (Member of the British Empire), but it was given to him, a least likely person. For people who have no might, God increases their strength and gives power to the weak. Maybe you can't say no to some habits, but God will give you power today, and then you will wake up one morning and say no. Maybe you have been struggling with alcohol quietly, sneaking, and drinking, and nobody knows. Perhaps you smoke and then wash your hand, and you use a nice-smelling perfume to cover the smell. God is ready to take all the least-likely out of their shell so that they will begin to do the almighty things. God is ready to increase the strength of those who have no strength for you to do the almighty things.

How does God bring these things to pass?

A. GOD WORKS ON US

Act 1:8 says, *"But ye shall receive power, after that the Holy Ghost is come upon you: and ye shall be witnesses unto me both in Jerusalem, and in all Judaea, and in Samaria, and unto the uttermost part of the earth."*

Let nobody deceive you that you have no power. You've got the power of the Holy Ghost. Let the Holy Ghost work through you. You've got to let Him work. God works on us every time, and as you read this book, God is working on you. God is working on our attitudes, the words we speak, our activities, marriage, ministry, businesses, family, and finances. He is working on your spouse, children, pastor, and congregation. God is working. Because if God doesn't work, there is no way that divine power can be activated—the power to get wealth, power to lay hold on serpents, snakes, scorpions, curses, and evil. The power of the Holy Spirit is impossible if God doesn't work on you. Also, Ezekiel chapter 36:25 says God works by sprinkling clean water on us so He can wash us.

"Then will I sprinkle clean water upon you, and ye shall be clean: from all your filthiness, and from all your idols, will I cleanse you" (Ezekiel 36:25).

And in Deuteronomy 34:7 Moses was one hundred and twenty years old when he died. His eyes were not dim nor his natural vigor diminished. The Scripture says God worked on Moses. He worked on every situation of his life, and God is also working on our insecurities. He hasn't given you the spirit of fear, but He has given you the spirit of power, love, and a sound mind. God is working; He is working!

B. GOD WORKS IN US

Being confident of this very thing, that he which hath begun a good work in you will perform it until the day of Jesus Christ (Philippians 1:6).

Maybe there are foul stenches coming from you; perhaps you have a body or mouth odour. You may even have some things that are not all right, and everything looks chaotic. For example, people can't come near you when you talk; just know God can work in you no matter your situation.

For it is God which worketh in you both to will and to do of his good pleasure (Philippians 2:13).

Anybody who desires to do God's will wants to do His good pleasure. Allow God to work in you! Most time, when God is working in us, we all complain. You may say *I don't know why I am going through all this*, but go through it first and see for yourself later on. Job said when I am tested, I shall come forth as gold. Gold is precious, but most of us just want to wear it. We didn't know what gold went through. It passed through fire for it to be polished, and then after polishing, the Italians put it in the market, and now you must queue to buy it. It doesn't matter how much it costs since you want it. Gold is very precious! When you are looking for pearls, it is very precious. You need to reach the sea to get that oyster and then peel the oyster. You scratch it to bring out that golden and special ornament out. It is very precious. When I am tested, I will come forth as gold. You are going through some things right now, murmuring and complaining. Get your focus right, right now, and say *when I am tested, I will come forth as gold*. Everything...the sufferings of this moment are not worth to be compared with the glory that will be revealed.

For I reckon that the sufferings of this present time are not worthy to be compared with the glory which shall be revealed in us (Romans 8:18).

There is glory coming; money cannot buy this glory. The glory will come upon you; it is coming upon your church.

C. GOD WORKS FOR US

Many people say *let me do it myself* when God is working for them. *I will rather do it myself*. God said *forget it, let me work for you*.

And Moses said unto the people, Fear ye not, stand still, and see the salvation of the LORD, which he will shew to you to day: for the Egyptians whom ye have seen to day, ye shall see them again no more for ever. The LORD shall fight for you, and ye shall hold your peace (Exodus 14:13-14).

In 2 Chronicles chapter 20, Jehoshaphat was faced with the wall with the three kings, and suddenly, he said *God, our eyes are on you. We don't know what to do.* God says, *step back; you don't need to fight any battle. This battle belongs to Me.* What do we see next? The Bible says in Proverbs 21:1, *the king's heart is in the hand of the LORD, as the rivers of water: he turneth it whithersoever he will.*

There was this young brother on a UK student visa, and his student visa had one month left. So, he decided to go for a renewal at the Home Office. This was 1998, thereabout. The laws were pretty harsh and harsher than they are right now. If it is a student visa for one month, they will give you your one month. If it is six months, they will give you your six months, and that is all. All this regulation and all haven't come around that time; things were strict at the Home Office with all these visas, and he said *before I go, I need prayer.* Proverbs 21:1 was used, and we declared and concluded that whoever you meet at that place will favour your application, and everything shall go well. I bind their heart and spirit man to flow in favour with you right now the way God wants it to happen. And so he rose and left, and from there, he phoned and said: *I don't know how it happened that instead of giving me a one-year renewal, they have given me an indefinite stay.* This happened in 1998.

D. GOD IS WORKING WITH US

For whom he did foreknow, he also did predestinate to be conformed to the image of his Son, that he might be the firstborn among many brethren (Romans 8:29).

If God is for us, who can be against us? Such a person is yet to be born. If people help you, one day, they will tell the story and say we are the people who helped him. If they say that story and you get over it, they will collect everything they have done for you back. After they have taken it back, they will still go to the street and say, *see, we are the one who helped him, and we have taken everything back from him. We will see what will become of him now.* Let them wait to see what you will become. If God is for you: I prophesy to you, no human being can be against you in the name of Jesus Christ. Some people are small in how they do things and talk; you can already see that.

E. GOD WORKS THROUGH US

And by the hands of the apostles were many signs and wonders wrought among the people; (and they were all with one accord in Solomon's porch (Acts 5:12).

God works through the apostles in signs and wonders so that they go everywhere, declaring the counsel of the Lord. Why? Because God was working through them. He said these signs should follow them that believe: *in my name they shall cast out devils, lay hold on serpents, lay hands on the sick and they will recover.* He said *go into the entire world and preach the gospel, baptizing them in the name of the Father, Son, and the Holy Spirit, and lo, I will be with you.* When God goes with us, He starts working through us.

John 4 shows the story of the woman at Sychar. Jesus requested to draw water, and then the woman said, *you don't have anything to draw the water.* He said there is a water I have that you don't know. The woman replied, *give me that water.* Then He said, *before I give you, go and call your husband,* and she said, *well, I have no husband.* He confirmed it as true because the man she was living with was not her husband. Jesus said she had five husbands, and the woman perceived Him as a prophet. He said you say so. Afterwards, the woman gave her life to Christ and went to the entire city and called everybody. She said, *come, I have seen a man who told me all I did.*

Is this not the Christ? God worked through that woman. When we are in a church, great things happen because great people and workers make it happen. When we are in the Body of Christ, great churches are built by great church members and workers who regularly bring people to the church. Every month, they bring people to church, that is how a great church is built, and the Holy Spirit starts working on them. All these show that God is working through us.

F. GOD WORKS AMONG US

God is the author of our families. He is the one who binds us together with the cords of love that cannot be broken. When the enemy comes to tear the love apart, they don't succeed except on the feeble ones, the nonentity ones, and those who are wise in their own strength and eyes. However, when God wants to work amongst us, He binds us with the cords of love that cannot be broken. If anybody wants to operate out of that love, the serpent will bite. When people start working out of that love, envy comes in, jealousy books a room, hatred makes a reservation, and low self-esteem comes for a holiday. However, when you are within the boundary of that love, the blessings of God are yours.

CHAPTER 3

Rivers of Living Water

JOHN 7:37-39

In the last day, that great day of the feast, Jesus stood and cried, saying, If any man thirst, let him come unto me, and drink He that believeth on me, as the scripture hath said, out of his belly shall flow rivers of living water.

But this spake he of the Spirit, which they that believe on him should receive: for the Holy Ghost was not yet given; because that Jesus was not yet glorified.

ROMANS 8:26-27

Likewise the Spirit also helpeth our infirmities: for we know not what we should pray for as we ought: but the Spirit itself maketh intercession for us with groanings which cannot be uttered.

And he that searcheth the hearts knoweth what [is] the mind of the Spirit, because he maketh intercession for the saints according to the will of God.

We want to talk about the rivers of living waters today in this book. We can't do much prayer without the Holy Spirit in our lives. If the

Holy Spirit is not in you, your prayers can't last and go far. Your prayer can't be really watered down the way God wants it to go.

1. The Holy Spirit is like a fuel that powers the words of our mouth, carries them, and waters them.

He allows it not only to be recorded but to gain weight around it. He makes our prayers have weight. He is not only required, but He allows the word of God that is in you, which you have received because it is very strong, according to Hebrews 4:12:

For the word of God is quick, and powerful, and sharper than any two-edged sword, piercing even to the dividing asunder of soul and spirit, and of the joints and marrow, and is a discerner of the thoughts and intents of the heart.

When the word of God falls upon anything, it breaks it into pieces, as stated in the Bible: that is how strong and weighty God's word is, which is why you need to put the word of God in you.

2. The word of God in you is flamed to life by the Holy Spirit through prayers.

As you pray, the word of God in you becomes alive. It becomes quick and active in your life. The Holy Spirit allows your prayer to receive the hearing of God through His angels. When you are praying, angels are suddenly armed. They become empowered and active. When the Holy Spirit begins to take your prayers, He takes the word of God and brings it to life, giving you the desire, ability, and empowerment of angels. Prayer is crucial through the power of the Holy Spirit.

The Holy Spirit is not just for speaking in tongues but helps with many things needed to occur in your life. If you are born again and not filled with the Holy Spirit yet, it means you are not maximising your Christian life. You are not maximising the Spirit of God's existence in your life. You are also not maximising your spiritual potential, i.e. the opportunities God has given you. The Holy Spirit is like the seed of God, which allows you to do many things you cannot ordinarily do by yourself. So, the Holy Spirit begins to execute God's plan and purpose for your life on this earth as a Christian. So, as the Holy Spirit comes into your life, you receive power.

ACT 1:8

But ye shall receive power, after that the Holy Ghost is come upon you: and ye shall be witnesses unto me both in Jerusalem, and in all Judaea, and in Samaria, and unto the uttermost part of the earth.

You become like a wild ox because you are now anointed and empowered by the Holy Spirit. A Christian who does not have the Holy Spirit is very powerless. Demons easily influence and oppress them but do not possess them because the Spirit of God is now in them. Christians must not say they are possessed because Christ, the anointed one, has been deposited into their lives. Therefore, you are not empty but powerful. The power of God is in you but what can happen is that if the power of God is not activated, all other contrary power will come, which are the demons to oppress a Christian. You are far from oppression because the Spirit of the living God is depositing Himself in you right now. The power of God has been activated in you, and out of your belly flows rivers of living water. When rivers of living water start flowing in you, the manifestation of living water commences. When the Holy Spirit comes, it activates the anointing of God resident in you and starts working on and in you.

PHILIPPIANS 2:12-13

Wherefore, my beloved, as ye have always obeyed, not as in my presence only, but now much more in my absence, work out your own salvation with fear and trembling.

For it is God which worketh in you both to will and to do of his good pleasure.

As the Holy Spirit begins to work in you and uproot your entire personal attitude like someone digging a well, He is putting His own Spirit into you. He will continue doing that all the time, not just overnight or for one month, depending on how thirsty you are for the Holy Spirit. You can understand the Bible in one year with real consciousness and understanding, not reading and understanding what is happening. It is according to the amount of time you spend with God. If you spend more time with God, the faster it is for the Holy Spirit to overwhelm you, dominate you, and take over your spirit completely. But if you don't give more time to the Holy Spirit, His work might not appear on time in your life. When we spend time with God, the Holy Spirit fills us up according to the songwriter, *'Fill my cup, Lord'*. You don't have to just sing the song; enjoy the reality. The Holy Spirit is real, and He wants to activate that anointing and reality in our lives so that we can become the wild soldiers God ordained us to be.

Many of us fear too many things. When we see a demon operating somewhere, fear comes to the heart of so many people. There are many people with different fears. Some have the fear of tomorrow, fear of uncertainty, and fear of height, but fear will not be in your heart again when the Holy Spirit is activated in your life. You will be able to understand the spiritual context and complexity of who you are as a person, that you are not just a physical being, but a spiritual one. *"I am a spirit; I have a soul and live in a body"*. Even though people identify us by our physical bodies, we should not forget who we are.

When God is talking about rivers of living water, we are describing the outburst of the Holy Spirit in our spirit man. When you take a little squashed orange or blackcurrant and splash water upon it, it bursts and mixes up. It is just the same thing. The Holy Spirit in us activates and bursts open what is already sealed up inside us, and the power begins to gush out. It becomes the fruit of the Spirit, the gift of the Spirit, the manifestation of the Spirit, and the power of the Spirit. Have you ever heard of the part that stated that Jesus went in the power of the Spirit? The anointing we receive bursts out the Spirit we already received in our heart, the consciousness and reality of the anointing we received when we were born again. So, at salvation, when you called Jesus Christ to come into your heart and be your Lord and Saviour, He put His Spirit inside of you. His Spirit is His anointing, the power concentrated inside of you. When you are born again, God gives you a measure of faith, but God expects you to cultivate that faith so it can become big, and then you can move mountains. So, with the little deposit, the Holy Spirit wants to work on it so that He can burst loose and open His manifestation in your life; that is when the difference can only be seen in us.

The stream of living water will flow from within one who believes in Jesus. That is, they will have a continuous source of satisfaction that will produce life. A Christian is said to be dead when God's Spirit is not operating in such a person's life again. But if the power that wakes Jesus Christ from the dead be in you, it will quicken your mortal body. This means you will become alive in Christ, in worship, and in prayers. Sleeping during prayers is wrong and shouldn't be like that, especially when it has become a constant thing. When you are alive, the Spirit of the living Christ quickens your mortal body and keeps you alive. You become active as long as you are passionate and ready for spiritual things.

People are not supposed to remind you about praying and reading your Bible daily. You should also be reminded of fellowshipping with God and fasting. You should not only remember God in times of need. It is a fool that only remembers God in time of need, but a son and a daughter have a deeper fellowship with their Father every day because the Holy Spirit makes it happen.

He will keep the feet of his saints, and the wicked shall be silent in darkness; for by strength shall no man prevail (1 Samuel 2:9).

You can't do much with your own human strength, and until you plug yourself into the Holy Spirit and surrender to Him, telling Him to take your own weakness and activate the treasure of God in you, you won't experience quickening. When you are quickened and come alive, no devil can hinder you or put obstructions and stumbling blocks in your path.

The Scripture explains that the river of living water is the coming gift of the Holy Spirit. The Gift that pours Himself into our lives. This Spirit within a believer satisfies his need for God and provides his need with regeneration, guidance, and empowerment. When you see a Christian today whose life is upside down, he is a powerless Christian. A powerless Christian is a prayerless Christian, and a prayerless Christian is an unfulfilled life. You can't say you are born again without fruit. We need to see the kind of fruit you portray and show because the Bible says we shall know them by fruit. When you have the Holy Spirit in you, His fruit will allow you to be seen by the world. You don't need to announce your salvation to the world. They will see it as you portray your works and deeds, and it is the Holy Spirit who can allow that work to be seen and shown to the entire world.

Dominion is inside you but doesn't come out until the Holy Spirit activates it. It is the power over Satan, sickness, and every power of the enemy.

Behold, I give unto you power to tread on serpents and scorpions, and over all the power of the enemy: and nothing shall by any means hurt you (Luke 10:19).

There is dominion, power, anointing, and wisdom inside of you.

And there shall come forth a rod out of the stem of Jesse, and a Branch shall grow out of his roots:

And the spirit of the LORD shall rest upon him, the spirit of wisdom and understanding, the spirit of counsel and might, the spirit of knowledge and of the fear of the LORD;

And shall make him of quick understanding in the fear of the LORD: and he shall not judge after the sight of his eyes, neither reprove after the hearing of his ears: ((Isaiah 11:1-3).

There is the wisdom of God in you, and the Holy Spirit wants to activate it. There is so much in you that requires unlocking by the Holy Spirit, and we are equivalent to the guy whose father has a billion in the account and gave the ATM card without the PIN. God puts everything inside of us. The Holy Spirit is the PIN that we can use to access and release the anointing, power, wisdom, glory, grace, dominion, and everything we need in this world to turn it around and make it great for the Almighty God.

How to Activate Rivers of Living Water

We must be thirsty to drink from it: When you are thirsty, you look for water. The same thing applies here: God says you must be thirsty before this river can flow from you. This also means you desire it strongly and passionately. You get dehydrated when you don't drink liquid for a long time. The body cells begin to collapse and close up, and you start shutting down. You can't sweat. All the urea in the body can't come out because the water is supposed to flush them out. The result is that the person starts swelling up gradually, which is the same with the Holy Spirit. If you don't drink Him, you will be dehydrated, many things will pack up, and your spiritual system will shut down completely. There will be no avenue for manifestation, but the fact is that you are still born again but not living in the fullness and power of it. God said *I have given you power.*

How God anointed Jesus of Nazareth with the Holy Ghost and with power: who went about doing good, and healing all that were oppressed of the devil; for God was with him (Acts 10:38).

God said He had deposited power in you, but you see a sick person and can't even lay hands on them. The consciousness is not even in you. You see someone possessed by the devil, and instead of commanding the devil to go, you are going away in fear. This happens because the spiritual system has collapsed. There is trouble on the inside already. The moment a child of God begins to live in fear, something is wrong on the inside already. So, we need to be thirsty for living water so we can drink.

Blessed are they which do hunger and thirst after righteousness: for they shall be filled (Matthew 5:6).

We must believe in order to drink. After you begin to desire it and become thirsty and hungry for it, you must believe it can happen because if you don't believe it can occur, it will not happen. So, we must believe in order to drink.

But without faith it is impossible to please Him: for he that cometh to God must believe that he is, and that he is a rewarder of them that diligently seek him (Hebrews 11:6).

You can receive from the Lord when you believe in Him. We must drink to be satisfied: drink to your satisfaction and drink to the fullness. To drink Christ Jesus means to count on Him ultimately, desire Him, and read His word daily because you know that you are thirsty for Him. It is crying out passionately to Him for more of His Spirit. That is, drinking more to be satisfied, not just drinking occasionally. When something approaches as satisfaction, it comes as enjoyment. The Holy Spirit is not boring; He is enjoyable. You need to come to that point when you begin enjoying His presence. You don't need to do the same thing you are doing before; something needs to be different. You only need a little progress at a time in anything you do, and you need to be better than before. Nobody must remain at a particular point; your state must be better than before, even for God to testify to it.

As He said, *the glory of the latter house is greater than the former* should be your testimony. And when God begins to measure your faith and things around you, He needs to certify that this is my beloved son and daughter, in whom I am well pleased. He must be overwhelmed by their progress in their fellowship and work with Him. All these can come to be with the help of the Holy Spirit.

We must overflow to other people: other people around us must see that this Holy Spirit is really working in our lives, and they can see it through our fruits. God can give gifts to anybody, but fruits are important because they overflow to other people around you. Fruits differ from gifts. Many people have gifts but don't have the fruit. It is fruits that keep you for a long time; this same fruit builds your character. It is this same fruit that builds your life as a Christian. It is also fruits that make the devil come in one way and flee in seven ways. Anybody can desire a gift, and it is given, but fruits must be worked on by and through the Holy Spirit.

The fruit of the Spirit is love, joy, peace, longsuffering, gentleness, goodness, faith, Meekness, temperance: against such there is no law.

And they that are Christ's have crucified the flesh with the affections and lusts (Galatians 5:22-24).

When you want an overflow to other people, it must come through the fruit. As it is written: *by their fruit you shall know them*. When God called Abraham, He said to him that he should walk before Him and be perfect and raise all the blessings upon him and to his generations. What was God saying? God was telling him that He wants him to also pass over the blessing to other people, which overflows through his fruit because the seed is sown in him; therefore, it germinates, and the fruits are seen.

I am the true vine, and my Father is the husbandman. Every branch in me that beareth not fruit he taketh away: and every branch that beareth fruit, he purgeth it, that it may bring forth more fruit.

Now ye are clean through the word which I have spoken unto you.

Abide in me, and I in you. As the branch cannot bear fruit of itself, except it abide in the vine; no more can ye, except ye abide in me (John 15:1-4).

It is only branches that bear fruits. Therefore, you are the branches, Jesus is the vine, and the Father is the vinedresser. This means He is the owner of the vine.

I am the vine, ye are the branches; He that abideth in me, and I in him, the same bringeth forth much fruit: for without me ye can do nothing.

If a man abide not in me, he is cast forth as a branch, and is withered; and men gather them, and cast [them] into the fire, and they are burned.

If ye abide in me, and my words abide in you, ye shall ask what ye will, and it shall be done unto you (John 15:5-7).

It is the word of God in you that the Holy Spirit flames to life. The Holy Spirit has nothing to flame out if nothing is in you. And whatever you ask Him through the word as it is recorded that the Holy Spirit helps our infirmity. He allows us to flame our requests through prayer, and then answers come. He also helps with our weaknesses. All this comes to be by the flow from the rivers of living water.

Herein is my Father glorified, that ye bear much fruit; so shall ye be my disciples.

As the Father hath loved me, so have I loved you: continue ye in my love.

If ye keep my commandments, ye shall abide in my love; even as I have kept my Father's commandments, and abide in his love.

These things have I spoken unto you, that my joy might remain in you, and [that] your joy might be full (John 15:8-11).

As everything becomes clearer to us now, we must overcome through our fruits. If you are not overflowing, it means you are not bearing any fruits, and when you are not bearing any fruit, it shows that the Holy Spirit is not operating and working in your life. It does not mean you don't have, but you are not maximising His presence. All you need to do is to tell Him to dominate and fill you every day, and the Holy Spirit wants to blow you up. The Holy Spirit will blow you up, and the whole world will see you and witness the power of God and the fruit of the Holy Spirit in your life.

CHAPTER 4

Direct Dial with God

"*C*all to Me, and I will answer you, and show you great and mighty things, which you do not know." Jeremiah 33:3

Many of us only call God when we are in trouble and have problems. Some people don't call Him unless somebody advises them to call Him. Others don't call Him because they are out of credit, and some of us flash Him, and He is embarrassed. Just as you dial your phone daily, God wants you to dial Him every time. His access code is very open. I want to show you in the Scripture how we can revolutionise our communication with God. It will help our relationship with God and help our prayer life. It will also help us to become stronger and better Christians.

And he spake a parable unto them to this end, that men ought always to pray, and not to faint; Saying, There was in a city a judge, which feared not God, neither regarded man: And there was a widow in that city; and she came unto him, saying, Avenge me of mine adversary. And he would not for a while: but afterward he said within himself, Though I fear not God, nor regard man; Yet because this widow troubleth me, I will avenge her, lest by her continual coming she weary me. And the Lord said, Hear what the unjust judge saith. And shall not God avenge his own elect, which cry day and night unto him, though he bear long with them? I tell you that he will avenge them speedily. Nevertheless when the Son of man cometh, shall he find faith on the earth? (Luke 18:1-8).

Direct dial! Just as you dial your phone daily, God wants you to have a direct dial to Him every day. His phone is very open, and it is unlimited and free. You don't need to be on any tariff or provider; it is just between you and Him. God is open, and all He wants you to do is stand wherever you are, and there is no specification of where you should be before you can call Him. You can be in the cave, on the mountaintop, in the car, walking on the street, on a football field, on a tennis court, on a golf court, or anywhere. There is no restriction to where you can access God.

Looking at this woman's story, she kept coming to the judge every day and knocking on the door, saying, *avenge me of my enemies*. That wasn't a repetitive prayer but a prayer of her desire, and she kept praying until she got her heart's desire. A prayer of repetition is different. A prayer of repetition is just a prayer of curiosity, making yourself look good before the person you are praying to. It makes everyone around you feel you know what you are doing and can pray. A prayer of repetition is not a prayer from the heart but a prayer of showing off. However, this woman wasn't showing off but meant business as she really had many enemies. Sickness is an enemy; poverty is another enemy, and not making progress as we are supposed to make it an enemy. Opposition is an enemy; diseases, ailments, afflictions, generational problems, Satan, and the flesh, are all our enemies.

So, when we talk about enemies, don't look at any human being as your enemy. We all have enemies and won't win battles until we understand and know the true enemy. For example, if your flesh is your enemy and it is pushing you to do many things, and you don't know, that means you are ignorant of a particular fact and won't be able to fight for victory in that area. And, until you begin to get victory over your flesh to a certain level in all those areas, you won't be able to get victory in all other areas. You might bind and loose so many things, and they will not be bound or loose because you are not winning the war against the first enemy—the flesh. My advice to you is to recognise the right enemy before it is too late and stop fighting the wrong one. This woman kept going to the judge who had no regard for man nor God, but he said something: *if I don't regard man nor God, but because this widow troubles me, I will do what she says.* The same way the story of yourself and God goes.

Prayer is communication between you and God. You are having communication, just as you are communicating with the other person on the other side of the phone, waiting to hear their voice and not just continuing talking without a reply. You give leverage for the other person to talk back as you are talking: the same goes for prayer. Most of us pick up the phone and complain and drop the phone without receiving a reply. That means you just talked and did not communicate. Paul summarised it as beating the air with our fists. Nothing will be done at the end when you have just talked to yourself without communicating because you did not approach His throne and presence the right way. Can you imagine yourself being ushered into Buckingham palace and the queen sitting on the throne, and all you did was just complain about what the councillors and the MPs are doing? What will happen next is that the palace guard will restrain you first and then throw you out because that is not the protocol for entering the palace. So, there is a protocol for entering God's presence.

There is a protocol for entering God's presence. The Bible says we should enter His gate with thanksgiving and His court with praise: that is the protocol to enter the presence of God.

A Psalm of David, when he changed his behaviour before Abimelech; who drove him away, and he departed. "I will bless the LORD at all times: his praise [shall] continually [be] in my mouth" (Psalm 34:1).

Enter His gate with thanksgiving so that the gate will open, and when the gate opens, you go into His court, and when you enter the court with praise, this means you are thanking Him for what He has done. On the other hand, praise means you are praising Him for who He is. Thank Him for creating the earth because without the earth being here, you won't be here. Thank Him because you have life, and because you have life, you have hope, and because you have hope, your tomorrow will be bright. Appreciate Him for everything because He has not held anything back. Thank Him for yet unanswered prayers because I know they will be answered. Then go into His court with praise; you are praising Him for who He is.

He is the King of kings and the Lord of lords, and when praising somebody, you are smiling, rejoicing, and excited. If somebody is praising you and frowning, you tend not to believe what the person is saying. Your composure, how you look, and your attitude become different. Anytime you enter the court with praises, you enter with the way you look with the attitude of simplicity, with the laughter of joy. Anytime you enter His court with praises, there is joy. The emphasis is that there must be joy in your heart, then everything will become possible for you, and you'll come into the consciousness of His presence. You'll access the consciousness of who He is as you come into His presence, knowing there is a God here. The fear of God will be in your heart, and the consciousness that He is present will be in you. Also, knowing and understanding He is around you makes you have confidence in Him.

You are not just rushing into His presence, getting crazy, frustrated, downloading His plans and running out again. You are not doing like that. The position of your state will not change like that. In His presence, we prayed with thanksgiving and His court with praise. These two things have loosened you up to a certain extent. It has relaxed you and taken some tension out of you. You can't pretend in God's presence; you will be real in His presence. I pray that the Holy Spirit will do surgery in our hearts and we will understand more about God.

Prayer is about trusting God to do His own will in your life and not your own will, or else, it will look like we are just giving the list of our needs to God and when we do that, there is no respect for God like that. When we pray, everything we pray to God must be in accordance with His will.

"And be not conformed to this world: but be ye transformed by the renewing of your mind, that ye may prove what [is] that good, and acceptable, and perfect, will of God" (Romans 12:2).

The will of God must be done in our lives; God is not interested in doing your own will. He is interested in you doing His will. Prayer is locating what God says and saying it back to Him so that He can make good His promise because whatever God says is His promise. Without locating what He says, you are playing on an empty tank, which is the assurance we have in finding what He says.

"And this is the confidence that we have in him, that, if we ask any thing according to his will, he heareth us" (1 John 5:14).

Then you go to the next level: worship.

Psalm 138:2: *"I will worship toward thy holy temple, and praise thy name for thy lovingkindness and for thy truth: for thou hast magnified thy word above all thy name."*

I will celebrate because you have magnified your word above your name. Can you see the importance of you locating what He has said? The word of God is crucial in prayer. It is telling you in the verse above that the word is important. Also, you first receive His word, and when you have received His word, you top it up with His name. He said what comes next as a protocol apart from thanksgiving, praises, and worship is finding God's word. When you find God's word, you can now top it with my name. When you mention the name of Jesus without the word, there must be something you will be armed with. You must arm yourself with the word of God and then fire the missile, which is God's word.

Call unto me, and I will answer thee, and shew thee great and mighty things, which thou knowest not (Jeremiah 33:3).

You go to God for Him to show you what you don't know, do what you can't do, sort you out in ways you can't sort yourself out, and to know His counsel for your life because if you know it, you won't go to Him. He is the only one with the dossier of your life on His desk twenty-four hours daily. His plan for our lives every day is all in His hand, not the hand of Satan. God wants to work in agreement with you. Only you have to make that plan come to pass, with only you involved and no other person. If God will help you, it is in His hand when you call on Him. It is also your responsibility to reciprocate and do according to His will. Then, things get done. It is not in Satan's hands. Many of us are binding Satan too much. When you bound him yesterday, was he loosed today? Your destiny is in the hands of God, and you have a duty to work it out and make it happen.

However, it will not become a reality if we don't work it out to make it happen and then play the blame game. Some of us blame Satan for our misfortune, despite God saying we should approach Him, and He will show us great and mighty things. Anything great is not ordinary, and it is usually massive. It means you are rediscovering who you are in God. There are too many things we don't know, and what you don't know can kill you. There are many things we don't know as Christians that we are not asking God to show us. I pray that God lightens your heart and you will not sleep the sleep of death. When God enlightens you, what He has already prepared, declared, said, planned, and programmed about you will be revealed to you. So many people give up because they have not seen their future and asked God to show them, and it is not only about heaven. Heaven is our final destination, absent from the earth and present with the Lord, where you live forever when you die on this earth. It's like you have just slept and are absent from the world but present with the Lord. In fact, the present life and eternity are what we are concerned about and what we should get right. The A-Z is already planned.

A was when you were born, and Z is eternity. Between A-B is what God already planned, and between the B-Y is where the tough job is. It is in-between that you get born again, marry, have children, and so on. Also, this is where the complications are and the area we don't get right. However, if you understand the power of a direct dial with God, that will be a direct boost for your life so that He can show you great and mighty things you don't know. There are great and mighty things we don't know, which is why we give up easily, start and don't finish. We blame this and that, become quitters, don't win, become so limited in our thinking, and live in unforgiveness, wrath, bitterness, and anger when we haven't seen what God has already planned and programmed for our lives.

"Behold, the days come, saith the LORD, that I will perform that good thing which I have promised unto the house of Israel and to the house of Judah" (Jeremiah 33:14).

"For thou, O LORD of hosts, God of Israel, hast revealed to thy servant, saying, I will build thee an house: therefore hath thy servant found in his heart to pray this prayer unto thee" (2 Samuel 7:27).

David here received the promise and prayed it back to God. Often, many of us receive the promise, and then we just sit down and say *God has already promised.* No! We are supposed to find it in our hearts to pray about it.

A blind man came to Jesus Christ and stood before Him, and Jesus asked him what he wanted. The point is, was Jesus not aware the man was blind? Yes, He was, but since He knew he was blind, why can't He heal him instead of asking first? However, all Jesus did was give him an opportunity to ask for what he wanted. That is exactly what God is looking for. He is tired of our murmuring, complaining, blame game, prayerlessness, slothfulness, and lukewarmness. He said, *find it in your heart to pray the promise back to me,* but if you don't know the Scripture, you will keep blaming God and say God is wicked. But for the accuracy and the efficacy of the word of God to come to pass in our lives, consider this verse:

So shall my word be that goeth forth out of my mouth: it shall not return unto me void, but it shall accomplish that which I please, and it shall prosper [in the thing] whereto I sent it (Isaiah 55:11).

So, all Jesus Christ did was to send the word and the blind man replied that I may see. All Jesus Christ said was that He should see. It was not the other way round because the scriptures must not be broken. He has magnified His word above His name. After today, there must be a revolution, and you must learn how to pray. How will you understand what His promises are and what He says?

Study to shew thyself approved unto God, a workman that needeth not to be ashamed, rightly dividing the word of truth (2 Timothy 2:15).

God is saying I want you to learn the word of God. My words are my promises, and I want you to learn them from what I say. It is through my word you will be sanctified, separated, and empowered. You will know my promises, come to that reality, and be able to access what I have said.

The promise, which is the word of God, is like a cheque you take to the bank, knowing full well that your father has money on the account. Then you sign the cheque and present it to the cashier, and you are confident that money is coming out. God doesn't use bank cheques; He already has the resources provided, and all you need to do is to get the word of God which is now the cheque. Say it, which is signing it, because it will be returned when not signed. He said this is the cheque, write the amount you desire according to His word and when you have prayed, believe and send it back to me, and then you get the money out. Then the promise is fulfilled.

And now, O Lord GOD, thou art that God, and thy words be true, and thou hast promised this goodness unto thy servant: (2 Samuel 7:28).

That by two immutable things, in which [it was] impossible for God to lie, we might have a strong consolation, who have fled for refuge to lay hold upon the hope set before us: (Hebrew 6:18).

What God has promised is what He will deliver. He will not deliver the opposite of what He had promised.

Thus saith the LORD, the Holy One of Israel, and his Maker, Ask me of things to come concerning my sons, and concerning the work of my hands command ye me (Isaiah 45:11).

If you find the word, you command Him according to the works of His hand. But if you do not find it, you have nothing to order, and it will be like a crime when you are ordering Him without the revelation of His word. This means we ask God with boldness.

CHAPTER 5

Baptism of the Holy Spirit

Every Christian must understand who the Holy Spirit is, how you can access Him, what happens when He comes into your life, what occurs if you don't have Him, and what happens when you have the Him.

And he said unto them, Go ye into all the world, and preach the gospel to every creature. He that believeth and is baptized shall be saved; but he that believeth not shall be damned. And these signs shall follow them that believe; in my name shall they cast out devils; they shall speak with new tongues; they shall take up serpents; and if they drink any deadly thing, it shall not hurt them; they shall lay hands on the sick, and they shall recover. So then after the Lord had spoken unto them, he was received up into heaven, and sat on the right hand of God. And they went forth, and preached everywhere, the Lord working with them, and confirming the word with signs following. Amen (Mark 16:15-20).

It is necessary for the Holy Spirit to work together with us for several reasons. It is important the Holy Spirit works in us. As Christians, who are born again, many things separate you from every other human being you find on the face of the earth. You are no longer under the control of the god of this world, Satan. When you become born again, you have come under the Almighty God's control, management, directive, protection, and Lordship. When the Almighty God becomes your manager and the director of your life, He helps you as He puts His own chip inside you.

Now, when you have your mobile phone, what you put inside it to make it work for you is a sim card, and there is a battery that you charge up. When you charge the battery, your phone can now begin to connect and do what it is supposed to do. The sim card allows you access to the network, allowing you to maximise and use your phone. The same thing goes for the remote control. There is something in the remote control that connects you to the machine it directs.

In the same way, God has put the Holy Spirit in us to help and direct us in the affairs of our lives because we are now under His control. We are now under His Lordship, management, influence, and power. So, God is the one who leads and directs us.

"For as many as are led by the Spirit of God, they are the sons of God" (Romans 8:14).

The sons in the above Bible verse mean male and female. Any time the Bible talks about this, it refers to both the male and female, the children of the living God. These are sons and daughters of the living God. So, the Holy Spirit becomes the navigator for our lives. He becomes the compass of our souls and the one that empowers us to flow in the will and counsel of God. When we became born again, part of the thing God did was to put the seal of the Holy Spirit upon us. He placed the hedges and the boundaries of the Holy Spirit around our lives so that the Holy Spirit can become the effective tool and weapon that galvanises or pushes us into the way and the things of God. We were just like people who were lost in this world before, and now, we are saved and brought under the control of the good shepherd, the Almighty God. Hence, He is the one who now facilitates our lives and guides us, helping us into the place He wants us to get, into the life He wants us to live, the person He wants us to become, the things He wants us to have, and the accomplishment He wants us to achieve. The Holy Spirit now becomes the one that guides and leads us in that direction.

The steps of a [good] man are ordered by the LORD: and he delighteth in his way (Psalm 37:23).

Before, you were the one who ordered your steps, but right now, God begins to order your actions to make the right choices and decisions and to be in the right place, doing things right. Before, you were lost in your own thoughts and did things by yourself; that is why it is dangerous for a born-again Christian to still be lost in His own world. Your world now has become the world of our Lord Jesus Christ through the Holy Spirit, so He has jurisdiction. Therefore, He can make the most and the best out of your life.

The Holy Spirit work in us for several reasons:

1. Because He is our comforter.

"All things that the Father hath are mine: therefore said I, that he shall take of mine, and shall shew [it] unto you" (John 16:15).

And so, on this basis, He begins to help by keeping us out of limitations and bringing us into God's expectations.

2. Because God has chosen the foolish things of this world to confound the wise.

"But God hath chosen the foolish things of the world to confound the wise; and God hath chosen the weak things of the world to confound the things which are mighty" (1 Corinthians 1:27).

We who were destined for destruction, to be nobodies, cheap weaklings, and foolish people, God takes that foolish thing and puts His Spirit into it. It became the controller of the world. It became a world changer and people that witness to the whole world. It became people empowered to lay hands on the sick to recover. It became people that cast out devils and spoke with new tongues. It became people who lay hold on serpents and even witnessed to all the earth. We became such people. So, God took the ordinary, put His power in Him through the Holy Spirit, and made us extraordinary.

3. So that we can develop spiritually and achieve an ongoing renewal of our spirits by the Holy Spirit.

"Not by works of righteousness which we have done, but according to his mercy he saved us, by the washing of regeneration, and renewing of the Holy Ghost" (Titus 3:5).

Also,

"And be not conformed to this world: but be ye transformed by the renewing of your mind, that ye may prove what is that good, and acceptable, and perfect, will of God" (Romans 12:2).

There are three areas also where the Holy Spirit chooses to work with us. Let's consider them below.

In Our Witnessing

This is an outward display of His power through our witnessing. Witnessing to the world means preaching and bringing a message to the world. Through our witness, there is an outward display of His power. We must go into the world as the Bible commands and preach the gospel. However, how do you do that without the Holy Spirit? For sure, many won't do it. But the Holy Spirit chooses to work in that area because God says in Acts 1:8:

"But ye shall receive power, after that the Holy Ghost is come upon you: and ye shall be witnesses unto me both in Jerusalem, and in all Judaea, and in Samaria, and unto the uttermost part of the earth."

In the above Bible verse, Jerusalem is your immediate environment. Judea is the next place beyond your comfort zone (other areas you won't go to ordinarily), while Samaria is known as other towns and cities, and the uttermost part of the earth is known as other countries, other parts of the world. You receive power because the Holy Spirit becomes the administrator that helps our witness.

In Our Worship

"Saying, Give me also this power, that on whomsoever I lay hands, he may receive the Holy Ghost" (Acts 8:19).

Here, the demonstration is uniquely to believers accomplished by our languages in our worship, as said in John 4:23-24:

"But the hour cometh, and now is, when the true worshippers shall worship the Father in spirit and in truth: for the Father seeketh such to worship him. God [is] a Spirit: and they that worship him must worship [him] in spirit and in truth."

It is impossible to worship God in truth and in spirit without the Holy Spirit. It will be a sacrifice of unrighteousness and of the lips. However, when the Holy Spirit comes, He allows us to express ourselves in worship to God, in appreciating God, in honour, in glorifying God, in making us not to feel empty but letting us understand that we are partakers of divine nature. We are heavenly beings; we are the children of the living God; we are not inferior; we are not hopeless; we are not sinners, but we come to our Father lifting up holy hands. The Holy Spirit helps us in our worship as we worship God so that we can open up our hearts just as we are, not thinking of our unrighteousness or the reason we are not qualified to worship God.

In Our Praying

He helps us in our witness, worship, and prayers, which energises our faith. If you don't pray, your faith can never be energised. When you pray, your faith is energised and when you study the word of God, your faith increases. What energises your faith is prayer, and what increases your faith is the word of God. If you don't pray, your faith will have no energy. It will just stay there dormant, alone, useless, and hopeless, not accomplishing anything. Those people become complainers and murmurers, but God said you have the tool and the key, yet you are not using it.

A Christian was kidnapped and locked up in a room, and they were asking for a ransom, but no ransom was coming. Evening came, and they were doing evil sacrifice and worship, and they said, *today, if no ransom comes, he will be offered for sacrifice*. Then, the Holy Spirit said *you are about to be offered for sacrifice; what will you do?* That is how best the Holy Spirit can go, because He is in you, and you have to nudge Him and put Him to work. He is just reminding him that He is still here, *use me*, which means open your mouth and begin to say things they don't understand. Then he summoned courage, and of course, somebody that has been kept in seclusion, beaten, with no food, frail, tired, feeling hopeless, and even feeling suicidal, the Holy Spirit said, *look, I am not going to let this one be sacrificed to idols. I have waited for too long.* So, the Holy Spirit kept reminding him that *I am still here; use me!*

The Holy Spirit will not act until you summon Him like the angel. Angels will not go on any assignment if you don't send them. So, he started praying in tongues, and his energy started coming. His faith became energised; he began to remember the word of God, started quoting scriptures, and the Holy Spirit got excited. The Holy Spirit was building His own spiritual fire that nobody saw as they were building their physical fire.

Suddenly, they stopped the drumming and said this man is saying something, and as he was saying that, we are becoming frozen. The fire is going out, and we don't know what he is saying. They became scared and said this man shouldn't be here. Who brought him here? So, they told him to walk away from there, and their fire going down suddenly exploded, which meant an explosion like a bomb had just happened, and they all ran away. But if he hadn't listened, and they frightened him so much he couldn't hear the nudge of the Holy Spirit, the Holy Spirit would never scream. He would just be whispering. He will be persistent, but He will never let you go. He helps our prayer, which energises our faith. So, He assists us in praying to God in tongues, as clearly seen in 1 Corinthians 14:2, where tongues is a language used to address God.

Areas Where We Need the Assistance of the Holy Spirit to Give Us Spiritual Words as We Pray

1. The Holy Spirit helps us get deeper into God's things.

So many Christians love and are convinced with a shallow life. Shallow life means I just pray a little prayer, sing some songs, read one verse of the Bible, become born again, and that is all. No life of power, fiery fire, boldness, authority, and dominion. They are just satisfied with the shallow level. The Holy Spirit takes you from shallowness into the deepness of the things of God.

2. The mysteries you speak are not directed to any man but God through His Holy Spirit.

3. We overcome the limitations of prayer from our personal understanding.

We overcome that limitation permanently because the Holy Spirit assists us in prayers, and praying in your understanding limits you to the realm of greatness and the realm of God. However, the Holy Spirit opens you up to the limitless realm of access to God.

4. The Holy Spirit edifies, builds, and strengthens us.

Now, what is this baptism of the Holy Spirit? Is it vital for us to have it? If it is not essential, the Lord Almighty won't talk about it. He would not make it important in His word as a sign to follow every believer, and He wouldn't only make it crucial that you speak to Him alone because God enjoys hearing you alone. It is like you don't value Him whenever you are not talking to Him. You don't treasure Him, you don't honour Him, or you don't appreciate His relationship with you. God enjoys hearing your voice. He enjoys it; He loves it so much. Any time you are not talking to Him, God gets upset. He is in a relationship with you, so He expects you to communicate every day and night because this is how He can prove Himself powerful in our lives. So, the baptism of the Holy Spirit is the enduement of God's power upon our spirit man to allow us move beyond our personal understanding, human limitations, and the ordinary, and step into the supernatural.

Peter was a sincerely nice, zealous, and good man who could not rightly define the plan and purpose of Jesus. When Jesus Christ said he was going to die, he said no! It is not possible; you won't die! And Jesus Christ said, who is that one who is standing against my commission, the reason I came into this earth? Then He said, *get behind me, Satan*. It was this same Jesus who came to this feeble man and said *Peter, after I have strengthened you, build others. After you have received the grace, feed the lamb; feed the sheep.* God knew that if He could only release His Holy Spirit upon these people, their lives would be turned around, and they would not only turn the world upside down, but they would also turn the world upright again for good. So, Peter, who once denied Jesus, did not see the commission of God in His life but became a man who now stood before a congregation and preached his heart out, and three thousand people came to the saving grace of the Lord Jesus Christ in one sitting. That is what the Holy Spirit can do, taking someone from the natural into a realm of the supernatural.

Why is the Church not flowing in the power God wants, and in a way God wants it to work in our lives? Many of us are born again and don't have the Holy Spirit. Many of us are born again but don't operate in the Holy Spirit. Many of us are born again, but we lack the power of the Holy Spirit. We lack the demonstration of that power in our lives. Hence, we are not seeing the signs and wonders God wants to activate in our time and generation. We are not seeing it. He said in Mark 16:17: *"And these signs shall follow them that believe; in my name shall they cast out devils; they shall speak with new tongues".*

There are many believers running away from demons. Any time you say *in the name of Jesus, every demonic power* becomes scared. Rather, you should be the one chasing out demons, not them chasing you. If the demons are chasing you, it means they have nothing in you to respect. You are born again, but you are not exercising that dominion, and instead of you exercising that dominion, they just see you and your emptiness, frailty, and low-key lifestyle. You do not understand what the power of the Holy Spirit is. They just take advantage of that, which is why Christians become oppressed by demons. That is where oppression comes from when you see demons beginning to chase you spiritually and physically everywhere.

He said: *"In my name if you drink any deadly thing it will not hurt you"*. There is no devil that can put poison into your drink if you have a proper revelation of the word of God. It won't even come; they won't bring food for you in your sleep. Haven't you seen people who ate in their sleep and later on start having different sicknesses and diseases they never had before in their lives? This is how the devil treats us when we become all these low-key Christians who don't appreciate the power of the Holy Spirit. The power of the Holy Spirit is yet to turn you loose, around, and make you volatile that every time they see you, they are scared and run.

"In my name they will speak with new tongues"; they will speak the mysteries of heaven. They will speak to God in mysteries and speak the language of angels, energising and strengthening their faith. They will be courageous and as bold as a lion. They will be able to pray into the future and years ahead. They will be able to cover years of ground in areas of their lives as they begin to grow spiritually and experience the power of the Holy Spirit.

He said, *"In my name they will lay hold on serpents".*

And the God of peace shall bruise Satan under your feet shortly. The grace of our Lord Jesus Christ [be] with you. Amen (Romans 16:20).

He said they would lay hold on serpents, which means they would match over serpents. You will bruise the head of Satan.

Behold, I give unto you power to tread on serpents and scorpions, and over all the power of the enemy: and nothing shall by any means hurt you (Luke 10:19).

This means you will lay hold on Satan and tell Satan *enough is enough. I take authority over you in the name of Jesus Christ.* At times, you need to demonstrate, practicalise, and visualise what you are praying about. When you visualise what you are praying about, you're gripping Satan's head, which provokes you to pray. It stirs you to unleash the power of the Holy Spirit upon that demonic experience. Visualise your prayer once in a while. When you pray that God's face should shine upon you, start seeing or visualising God's face coming upon yours.

But we all, with open face beholding as in a glass the glory of the Lord, are changed into the same image from glory to glory, even as by the Spirit of the Lord (2 Corinthians 3:18).

This means God put His own face over my own face. Moses came out from God's presence, and they saw His glory upon him. God put His own face over him, and they couldn't stay there. The glory was too powerful. You don't want to know what God's face looks like. Don't be too homiletical, political, and intellectual, saying *I want to know what the face of God looks like. Does it look like this person?* But just by faith, say, *Lord, put your face over my face so that when I appear anywhere, my appearing will be like the sight of the living God.* I'm teaching you something about working in dominion today because some people have turned back to ordinary things. People just look at you, and they don't see any difference. They don't see anything new about you. However, when you say, *Lord, put Your face to cover my face. Let Your face shine on me, oh God! Let me see Your glory.* They will see the glory of God upon you instead of your person.

What happens when the Holy Spirit comes on us? Or why do we need the baptism of the Holy Spirit?

a. The Holy Spirit comes on us so that we can receive His baptism with the initial evidence of speaking in tongues because Jesus said we could receive it so far we are believers.

And these signs shall follow them that believe; In my name shall they cast out devils; they shall speak with new tongues (Mark 16:17).

I can speak with new tongues after I am born again. I am baptised and have the evidence of speaking with new tongues to say the Holy Spirit has come.

b. Because Jesus believed that all that were present at His ascension needed the power to be witnesses, and because we are witnesses, we need to be endued with power from heaven.

And, being assembled together with them, commanded them that they should not depart from Jerusalem, but wait for the promise of the Father, which, [saith he], ye have heard of me.

For John truly baptized with water; but ye shall be baptized with the Holy Ghost not many days hence (Acts 1:4-5).

Because we are God's witnesses, we need and must be endued with power from on high.

c. Because the empowerment is for us to be witnesses and reach the uttermost part of the earth; therefore, tongues are not limited to our world and our people alone.

So, we need that empowerment through that baptism to go into all the world. On the day of Pentecost, everybody gathered, about 120 people. They started praying in the Holy Ghost, and some people came around and identified with what they were saying and said, *these people are speaking my country's language.* They asked how this was possible. *We all know all these people. How is it possible?* It's the power of the Holy Spirit.

When you become more exposed to the things of God, you will value the Holy Spirit more, especially when you are out of your comfort zone. You will value the appearance and the power of the Holy Spirit in your life as an individual. Now, because you are not overexposed, you don't do all you can to get out more in the things of God. We become limited, and so our understanding also becomes limited. Our lifestyle has also become limited; it's like we are caged in. It's like a shark in an aquarium. It doesn't thrive in an aquarium but in an ocean. Until you become conversant with the word, find yourself being convenient around people not from your nation, colour, race, or tribe. You will see the Holy Spirit more in action.

d. If we tarry for the promise of the Father, we too can receive because anybody that tarried or waited received.

And, behold, I send the promise of my Father upon you: but tarry ye in the city of Jerusalem, until ye be endued with power from on high (Luke 24:49).

e. Because these are the last days, at the time of the Messiah, you can know Him more as you receive the baptism of the Holy Spirit by speaking the same way they spoke on the day of Pentecost.

But this is that *which was spoken by the prophet Joel;*

And it shall come to pass in the last days, saith God, I will pour out of my Spirit upon all flesh: and your sons and your daughters shall prophesy, and your young men shall see visions, and your old men shall dream dreams:

And on my servants and on my handmaidens I will pour out in those days of my Spirit; and they shall prophesy:

And I will shew wonders in heaven above, and signs in the earth beneath; blood, and fire, and vapour of smoke:

The sun shall be turned into darkness, and the moon into blood, before that great and notable day of the Lord come:

And it shall come to pass, that whosoever shall call on the name of the Lord shall be saved.

Ye men of Israel, hear these words; Jesus of Nazareth, a man approved of God among you by miracles and wonders and signs, which God did by him in the midst of you, as ye yourselves also know:

Him, being delivered by the determinate counsel and foreknowledge of God, ye have taken, and by wicked hands have crucified and slain:

Whom God hath raised up, having loosed the pains of death: because it was not possible that he should be holden of it.

For David speaketh concerning him, I foresaw the Lord always before my face, for he is on my right hand, that I should not be moved:

Therefore did my heart rejoice, and my tongue was glad; moreover also my flesh shall rest in hope:

Because thou wilt not leave my soul in hell, neither wilt thou suffer thine Holy One to see corruption.

Thou hast made known to me the ways of life; thou shalt make me full of joy with thy countenance.

Men [and] brethren, let me freely speak unto you of the patriarch David, that he is both dead and buried, and his sepulchre is with us unto this day.

Therefore being a prophet, and knowing that God had sworn with an oath to him, that of the fruit of his loins, according to the flesh, he would raise up Christ to sit on his throne;

He seeing this before spake of the resurrection of Christ, that his soul was not left in hell, neither his flesh did see corruption. This Jesus hath God raised up, whereof we all are witnesses.

Therefore being by the right hand of God exalted, and having received of the Father the promise of the Holy Ghost, he hath shed forth this, which ye now see and hear.

For David is not ascended into the heavens: but he saith himself, The LORD said unto my Lord, Sit thou on my right hand, Until I make thy foes thy footstool.

Therefore let all the house of Israel know assuredly, that God hath made that same Jesus, whom ye have crucified, both Lord and Christ (Acts 2:16-36).

This scripture proves it. On the day of Pentecost, there was a cloven tongue of fire and a mighty rushing wind, and their spirit man became alive. Their act became open, and their mouths connected with their hearts, and they began to speak mysteries. Those are not what man can do, not what man can give, but what the Holy Spirit can do. It is a mystery. If it happened then, it could happen now, and it is a guarantee that if they needed it, we would need it now. These are still the end times of the Messiah's reign.

f. We, too, can receive the fullness of the Holy Spirit separately from the one we receive at conversion, because the one we receive at conversion is not enough.

We can receive the fullness of the Holy Spirit and commemorate the receiving of that fullness, which leads to our speaking in tongues. When you start speaking in tongues, it is a guarantee you have already received the fullness of the guarantee of the Holy Spirit. So, you are full of the Holy Spirit. You are not empty again. When you are born again, you are limited in the Holy Spirit. When we were born again, the Holy Spirit came through that empowerment of salvation to begin the work of regeneration in our lives because the difference has to be seen and known. We have to be regenerated, and the difference has to be noted. But after that, we are to receive the fullness of the Holy Spirit, so after being born again, don't wait for one year or two or more years before being filled with the Holy Spirit. You are to immediately ask for the fullness of the Holy Spirit.

I remember I became born again on the 7th of January, 1990, and they kept me there and said, there is something about you. They kept praying for me, and on the 10th, they organised a program and called it "The Holy Spirit". Just as it happened to Saul after Ananias took him and was praying for him for three days, it happened to me. On the third day, Paul just caught fire. The Holy Spirit came upon him and healed him of his blindness. His eyes were opened; the Holy Spirit came upon him, and that is why he said *I spoke in tongues more than you all*. The Holy Spirit came upon him, and he started speaking in tongues. He correlated the letter when he was writing 1 Corinthians 14.

I thank my God, I speak with tongues more than ye all: (1 Corinthians 14:18).

Because that power came upon him so much recklessly, he left Ananias' house to become a prophet to the nations. That is what we need now. We need to become radical Christians, not all these Christians who are still oppressed by one thing or the other. Christians who don't have money to come to church, nor have bus fare and don't want to come to church. Christians who don't want to follow God again, who have no guarantee for answers to their prayers and then feel God is not there again. Christians who feel church, reading the Bible, and praying are just casual stuff.

When the Holy Spirit comes upon you in full measure, you will hunger for that word of God. You will hunger for prayer because it becomes your life. Can you imagine not sleeping for three days, four days, and so on? What will happen? One of our pastors, Pastor Leke Sanusi, couldn't sleep for twenty-five days some years ago. Then he said *no, I have to sleep*. They prayed for him and laid hands on him; still, no sleep until he checked with his family and came into seclusion. He said *we have prayed, we have laid hands, but you will stay in this room and I will stay in the other, and I will worship*. He started worshipping the Holy Spirit: this was about twenty years ago. He started worshipping, and suddenly, he felt like the windows and doors were opened, and a mighty rushing wind just came in over him. He fell and slept after twenty-five days; that is the work of the Holy Spirit. If you don't pray and study the Bible, it is death.

Can you imagine not having air to breathe? It is the same thing, and that is what the Holy Spirit does. And when you confirm the fullness of that measure by speaking in tongues, nobody needs to tell you again. Even if people offend you, you don't care because you don't want to quench or grieve the Holy Spirit. The Holy Spirit doesn't stay in a place of strife, unforgiveness, bitterness, evil communication, slanders, gossip, and everything malicious.

The Holy Spirit does not strive with people. He doesn't work with strife. He will not stay there. So, when people are engaging in that area, separate yourself and say *I will not lose the Holy Spirit*. This Holy Spirit is your life; whatever they say or do against you, don't let it bother you. Just protect the Holy Spirit in you so that He can give the fullness of that measure of the Spirit of God upon you, and your life will not diminish.

g. Because God is no respecter of persons, He gives His gift of the Holy Spirit to those He saves.

That gift came for the first time in Acts 10 upon Cornelius. He was a Gentile and Roman Centurion but feared God in his heart. He kept believing, praying, helping the poor, and assisting the needy, until one day, God said *your prayer and alms have come to me. I am sending Peter to you*, and the Holy Spirit came upon a Gentile and his entire household. They were slain in the Holy Spirit after they were saved. They were baptized not only in water but also in the Holy Spirit. The power of God came upon their lives, and they became transformed. If the Holy Spirit did that to Cornelius, He is no respecter of persons. He is here to give us the fullness of the Holy Spirit, with the evidence of speaking in tongues. It is important.

h. So that our infirmities and weaknesses can be removed.

Our infirmities are related to our prayer areas, and God can work together through His Holy Spirit in our lives.

Likewise the Spirit also helpeth our infirmities: for we know not what we should pray for as we ought: but the Spirit itself maketh intercession for us with groanings which cannot be uttered.

And he that searcheth the hearts knoweth what is the mind of the Spirit, because he maketh intercession for the saints according to the will of God (Romans 8:26-27).

i. We speak in tongues and function in the gifts of God because the Bible says God's gifts are irrevocable.

Therefore, the gifts and the callings of God are without repentance.

For the gifts and calling of God are without repentance (Romans 11:29).

j. Tongues will seize at rapture; prophecy and knowledge will continue, but Jesus requires us to keep praying in tongues until He comes, till we see Him face to face. So, He says we should pray in the Spirit with all prayer and supplications.

Praying always with all prayer and supplication in the Spirit, and watching thereunto with all perseverance and supplication for all saints; (Ephesians 6:18).

If I pray in an unknown tongue, my spirit prays, but my understanding is unfruitful, which means I can't do it. It's not the same thing. Praying in understanding is different from praying in the Spirit. They are of different dimensions. Whenever I pray in the Spirit, my understanding is subdued because praying in understanding is different from praying in the Spirit. Praying in understanding is for you to understand. When you pray in the Spirit, it is not in your understanding. You are praying to God; it is a mystery! And my understanding is unfruitful. It is only God who understands what I'm praying about. Speaking in tongues is not something for you to make noise about and let the whole world know, and then you pose as if you are better than every other person in the church. We are encouraged to pray loud but not with nepotism. It is not with a particular complex formula; it is just praying to God Almighty.

When we are baptized in the Holy Spirit, some things happen in our lives. These are the things God says it is important for you to understand. He wants you to have that empowerment so you can pray in the Spirit and talk to Him directly. There are life cases where you need to activate your faith, like the earlier example of the kidnapped man. He needed to go through that route, and going through the route will bring you into a stage where the enemy doesn't even understand. The enemy doesn't understand what you are saying when you pray in the Spirit, in tongues, and with your heart. The enemy is confounded because you are praying to God, who understands what you are praying about. After all, He is the one who gave you that empowerment in the first place. So, every born-again person needs to be baptized in the Holy Spirit.

Jesus advised us to keep praying with all prayers and supplications until He comes. So, when the rapture comes, tongues will seize, and everything else continues. But before it stops, God wants us to pray in the Spirit and receive the Holy Spirit as the Cornelius family received it, as the Apostles of old received it, like Paul the Apostle received it. For everyone who receives it, there is an explosion in their lives. Their lives turned around for the best. What makes you think you won't need it? Jesus could not do anything in ministry until the Holy Spirit came upon Him. The Holy Spirit had to come upon Jesus. If Jesus needs it, what makes you and I think we won't need it? We just listen to the world philosophers and scientists who would tell us there is no need for us to have it. They are talking you out of your own fullness and empowerment in the Holy Spirit. Some people write books, some preach on TV, and others come against many things. They have their own doctrine; all these are wrong. Base your own life on what God says. Go and study these scriptures given here and meditate on them. Don't listen to all these books and anything contradicting what God says. It is heresy! It is wrong! It is completely wrong and out of place! And it is allowing the devil to put a blanket over our faces so that we don't know the truth, and the truth makes us free.

The Holy Spirit makes you enjoy your relationship with God more. The Holy Spirit will open your mind to a new level of understanding. The Holy Spirit will open your spirit man so that you can start seeing the future and see what God has already planned. What He is planning and what He is about to do, the Holy Spirit will allow the wisdom of God to furnish your life so that when you speak, people will wonder where you get it from. They will marvel about where you heard that from, how you managed, and how you got all this. Then you say it is the Holy Spirit, and today, I decree that uncommon change in the name of Jesus Christ. I decree that uncommon transformation over your spirit man, in the name of Jesus Christ.

CHAPTER 6

Trusting God's Plan for Your Life

But the path of the just is as the shining light, that shineth more and more unto the perfect day (Proverbs 4:18).

God has a plan for my life and wants me to know His plans so that my life can accelerate and lock into what He planned.

There are many plans in a man's heart, Nevertheless the Lord's counsel—that will stand (Proverbs 19:21; NKJV).

God's plan is not evil but good; it has positive outcomes.

For I know the plans I have for you," declares the Lord, "plans to prosper you and not to harm you, plans to give you hope and a future (Jeremiah 29:11; NIV).

I proceed to enjoy and flow in the plan according to God's leading, direction, and guidance.

The steps of a good man are ordered by the Lord, And He delights in his way (Psalm 37:23; NKJV).

Definition

God's plan is defined as a premeditated divine strategy of God designed to accomplish a righteous objective.

1. In other words, we need to,
2. Find a plan from God
3. Focus on the plan of God
4. Follow the plan of God
5. Be fruitful in the plan of God

The Lord brings the counsel of the nations to nothing; He makes the plans of the peoples of no effect. The counsel of the Lord stands forever, The plans of His heart to all generations (Psalm 33:10-11; NKJV).

Declaring the end from the beginning, And from ancient times things that are not yet done, Saying, 'My counsel shall stand, And I will do all My pleasure,' (Isaiah 46:10).

God's plans and purpose are to help mankind. Therefore, I must be willing to accept God's plan for my life so it will come to pass.

God also put principles in place to enable His plans to come to pass for my life.

Isaiah 55:8-9 (NKJV) shows us the ways of God:

"For My thoughts are not your thoughts, Nor are your ways My ways," says the Lord. "For as the heavens are higher than the earth, So are My ways higher than your ways, And My thoughts than your thoughts.

The Revelation of God's plan

God's plan is superior to mine. God is smarter than me. He knows the end from the beginning.

"I am the Alpha and the Omega, the Beginning and the End," says the Lord, "who is and who was and who is to come, the Almighty" (Revelations 1:8; NKJV).

We must rely on Him to get us through life and total destiny. He is the author and finisher of our faith.

Looking unto Jesus, the author and finisher of our faith, who for the joy that was set before Him endured the cross, despising the shame, and has sat down at the right hand of the throne of God (Hebrews 12:2; NKJV).

God gives us the strength to fulfil the plan.

So, when we talk about the revealed plan of God, let's consider the following:

1. God's plan is **INTENTIONAL** and purposeful.
2. God's plan is **INTIMATE**, which is the response of HIS love for us and the product of God's love.
3. God's plan is to **INCREASE** and bring divine increase into our lives because we are on His mind.
4. God's plan is an **IMPACTFUL** plan. It changes and enables us to make a difference in our lives and the world we live in today.
5. God's plan is **INDIVIDUAL**-based and tailor-made for each of us, which means it's unique to each person.
6. God's plan is an **INCORRUPTIBLE** plan, which means nothing can stop the plan. No giant, red sea, or devil can ever stop the plan of God.

How God reveals His plans

For this is the love of God, that we keep His commandments. And His commandments are not burdensome (1 John 5:3; NKJV).

The plan of God is for my benefit and to restructure my life to obey God because obedience to God is for my benefit.

1. SCRIPTURES reveal the plan of God.

The written word of God becomes a standard for my guidance in 2 Timothy 3:16. God's plan always agrees with the word of God.

2. The SPIRIT of God also reveals God's plan as seen in 1 Corinthians 2:9-10.

The personal voice of the Spirit of God on the inside speaks with the prophetic author, arms, and declarations.

3. Holy Ghost's plan is revealed by true angelic SUPERNATURAL visitation.

God send His angels to visit and speak to us and uncover mysteries that will line us up in life's journey.

4. God's plan is also revealed through the SAINTS and scriptural based people that God has placed in authority—apostles, prophets, evangelists, pastors, teachers, mature Christians, etc.

How God's Plans are Received

There is a plan of God for my life, and this is received through:

1. SALVATION

Received by grace from our Saviour, and I am saved by His grace.

For by grace you have been saved through faith, and that not of yourselves; it is the gift of God, (Ephesians 2:8; NKJV).

For all have sinned and fall short of the glory of God, being justified freely by His grace through the redemption that is in Christ Jesus, (Romans 3:23-24; NKJV).

2. SERVICE

God's plan is received through my service and partnership with Him.

For we are His workmanship, created in Christ Jesus for good works, which God prepared beforehand that we should walk in them (Ephesians 2:10).

God has equipped everyone with what the kingdom of God needs.

I, therefore, the prisoner of the Lord, beseech you to walk worthy of the calling with which you were called, (Ephesians 4:1; NKJV).

We are created to play our parts, no matter how small.

3. SUCCESS

God also has a plan for my success, salvation, and partnership with Him. He also has a plan for my success, so God wants me to prosper.

Beloved, I pray that you may prosper in all things and be in health, just as your soul prospers (3 John 2; NKJV).

Accepting the plan

To be able to embrace and accept God's plan for our lives, we need to trust God first.

Trust in God for the plan is highly essential.

There is a way that seems right to a man, But its end is the way of death (Proverbs 16:25; NKJV).

Trust in God comes through my fellowship with Him. The more I know God, the more I trust Him. For example, in John 5:5-8 (NKJV),

Now a certain man was there who had an infirmity of thirty-eight years. When Jesus saw him lying there, and knew that he already had been in that condition a long time, He said to him, "Do you want to be made well?" The sick man answered Him, "Sir, I have no man to put me into the pool when the water is stirred up; but while I am coming, another steps down before me." Jesus said to him, "Rise, take up your bed and walk."

That was a story of a man by the pool of Bethsaida. He needed God's word and plan for his life to be established and manifested.

Let's look at the issue at stake here:

1. He was **LAME** {had a handicap}.
2. He was **LAID** down, which means he depended on people to carry him everywhere.
3. He was **LEFT** alone and abandoned by people, government institutions, and family.
4. He was **LACKING**, which means he had to beg people to receive provision. So, He was begging people instead of looking out to God.
5. He was **LOOKED** for by Jesus to be able to declare God's plan for his life.
6. He was **LIFTED** up. God healed him, made him whole, and plugged him into God's plan for his life.

Therefore, in order to trust God, accept the plan and embrace the plan. We have to move beyond:

#disrespecting the plan

#resisting the plan totally

#rejecting the plan

AND

Move to get to the point of:

#Believing and receiving it.

#Have the boldness to respond to God's plan.

All to the glory of God

CHAPTER 7

Maximise Results Through Prayer

Then He spoke a parable to them, that men always ought to pray and not lose heart, (Luke 18:1).

LUKE 11:1-13; LUKE 18:1-8

The Holy Spirit teaches us what to pray and say (Luke 12:12).

The Holy Spirit helps us (Romans 8:26).

Lord, teach us to fight and train our fingers for war (Psalm 144:1).

Train my hands to battle and my fingers to bend irons (Psalm 18:34).

"Prayer... is the root, the fountain, the mother of a thousand blessings...

The potency of prayer has subdued the strength of fire. It has bridled the rage of lions...extinguished wars, appeased the elements, expelled demons, burst the chains of death, expanded the gates of heaven, healed diseases...rescued cities from destruction...and arrested the progress of the DESTRUCTION."

Maximise—achieve to the fullest capacity

How to maximise? Pray with blessing.

The sacrifice of the wicked is an abomination to the Lord, But the prayer of the upright is His delight (Proverbs 15:8; NKJV).

Pray with passion

And the hand of the Lord was with them, and a great number believed and turned to the Lord (Acts 11:21).

Antioch was transformed, becoming a distinguished Christian city and the springboard for Christian missions.

Pray to God

Prayer to God means having an audience with God. It means actually coming into God's presence—asking and receiving.

"And in that day you will ask Me nothing. Most assuredly, I say to you, whatever you ask the Father in My name He will give you (John 16:23; NKJV).

Pray together

There is even more power in praying together.

"Again I say to you that if two of you agree on earth concerning anything that they ask, it will be done for them by My Father in heaven (Matthew 18:19; NKJV).

Pray Strategically

In Acts 12, there are two reasons they might not have prayed at all. First, James had been killed (v.2). God had not answered their prayers for James; we don't know why. But it did not stop them from praying.

Second, Peter was arrested and jailed, and his situation seemed impossible. Their choice was either to give up praying or to pray strategically.

Pray for others

Job prayed for his friends.

And the Lord restored Job's losses when he prayed for his friends. Indeed the Lord gave Job twice as much as he had before

(Job 42:10; NKJV).

There are many types of prayer: worship, praise, thanksgiving, petition, and so on—but here, we read of intercessory prayer. They prayed for him because they loved him. An intercessory prayer is an act of love.

God's answer involved visions, angels, and chains falling off (Acts 12:6–9). Obstacles were removed. The guards did not bar the prisoners' escape, and the iron gate to the city opened in front of them (v.10).

This chapter opens with James dead, Peter in prison, and Herod triumphing. It closes with Herod dead, Peter freed, and the word of God triumphing.

Pray for wisdom & direction

James writes, *'If any of you lacks wisdom, you should ask God, who gives generously to all without finding fault, and it will be given to you'* (James 1:5; NKJV).

Why Pray?

Because of significance and importance of prayer to our spiritual life.

...but we will give ourselves continually to prayer and to the ministry of the word" (Acts 6:4; NKJV).

"In return for my love they are my accusers, But I give myself to prayer" (Psalm 109:4; NKJV).

As fuel to a car, prayer is nourishment to a spiritual life for effective living.

As human spirit to the body, so is prayer to our spiritual life.

Because praying doesn't come naturally, we must be taught to pray. Eating, breathing, and talking come naturally.

Now it came to pass, as He was praying in a certain place, when He ceased, that one of His disciples said to Him, "Lord, teach us to pray, as John also taught his disciples" (Luke 11:1; NKJV).

Prayer has various aspects. So, we must understand the power of each aspect.

Petition, Supplication, Thanksgiving.

Intercession, Agreement, Commitment.

Unity, Faith, etc.

Every place has a protocol of entry.

Be anxious for nothing, but in everything by prayer and supplication, with thanksgiving, let your requests be made known to God; (Philippians 4:6; NKJV)

Prayer is a weapon, both offensive and defensive.

"...praying always with all prayer and supplication in the Spirit, being watchful to this end with all perseverance and supplication for all the saints" (Ephesians 6:18; NKJV).

"Blessed be the Lord my Rock, Who trains my hands for war, And my fingers for battle" (Psalm 144:1; NKJV).

Because of inspiring testimonies and the life of achievements of those who prayed.

Daniel

"Now when Daniel knew that the writing was signed, he went home. And in his upper room, with his windows open toward Jerusalem, he knelt down on his knees three times that day, and prayed and gave thanks before his God, as was his custom since early days" (Daniel 6:10; NKJV).

Paul

"And it happened that the father of Publius lay sick of a fever and dysentery. Paul went in to him and prayed, and he laid his hands on him and healed him" (Acts 28:80; NKJV).

Jesus

Then Jesus came with them to a place called Gethsemane, and said to the disciples, "Sit here while I go and pray over there" (Matthew 26:36; NKJV).

Hezekiah

Faced with DESTROYER

Then Hezekiah prayed to the Lord, saying: (Isaiah 37:15; NKJV)

Faced with DEATH

Then Hezekiah turned his face toward the wall, and prayed to the Lord (Isaiah 38:2; NKJV)

3 Hebrew boys (Daniel 3:16-18).

Elijah (I Kings 18) Mount Carmel.

Jacob (Genesis 32) Wrestled.

Dismantle forces of Darkness, Wickedness, and Satanic Works

Having disarmed principalities and powers, He made a public spectacle of them, triumphing over them in it (Colossians 2:15; NKJV).

Because many of us don't know the potency and power of praying, adding a prayer curriculum to our lives will let everything out of place to be sharpened, hammered, panel-beaten, and sandpapered into the right place.

Many times, the problem is with our prayerlessness, not because:

- The devil has become stronger
- God has forgotten, rejected, neglected, or overlooked us (Heb. 13:5-6).
- We have sinned or become reckless; hence, we are now in trouble or a mess.

To fulfil your God-given destiny and maximise your life.

"The Spirit of the Lord is upon Me, Because He has anointed Me To preach the gospel to the poor; He has sent Me to heal the brokenhearted, To proclaim liberty to the captives And recovery of sight to the blind, To set at liberty those who are oppressed; (Luke 4:18; NKJV).

To stand with others in prayer, teach other people, and be a praying person.

Can two walk together, unless they are agreed? (Amos 3:3; NKJV).

Teach others

And the things that you have heard from me among many witnesses, commit these to faithful men who will be able to teach others also (2 Timothy 2:2; NKJV).

What Prayerlessness causes

1. If your prayer bank is empty or low, you'll be vulnerable, and your destiny will be insecure.

2. Prayerlessness is an attempt to dethrone God. Prayerlessness means you can do without God. But no one can do without God.

3. The devil has no fear for a Christian who doesn't pray. Does the devil know your identity in the spirit realm? (Referencing sons of Sceva).

4. You will be very barren of the anointing. Your prayerless lifestyle is the reason you're not anointed. Your gifts and potential will lie dormant without prayer.

5. Delay in marriage, getting admission, and fulfilling destiny are results of prayerlessness.

6. A prayerless Christian will backslide and compromise easily. Prayer strengthens your conviction and consecration.

7. You will not be useful to your generation without a prayer life. It takes a lifestyle of prayer to bless your generations.

CHAPTER 8

Coming Out Stronger

I tremble and fear before the God of Daniel. For He is the living make a decree that in every dominion of my kingdom men must God, And steadfast forever; His kingdom is the one which shall not be destroyed, And His dominion shall endure to the end. He delivers and rescues, And He works signs and wonders In heaven and on earth, Who has delivered Daniel from the power of the lions (Daniel 6:26-27; NKJV).

To come out stronger means:

#Become better

#To improve quality

#Have a better lease on life

#Gain more power

#Better version

#Undamaged

- The end or outcome of a matter is better than the beginning or when you started.

The end of a thing is better than its beginning; The patient in spirit is better than the proud in spirit (Ecclesiastes 7:8; NKJV).

- You've gained more with great increase. Things are not as it was before or used to be.

Though your beginning was small, Yet your latter end would increase abundantly (Job 8:7; NKJV).

- You've fought a good fight of faith. You went, saw, fought, and conquered.
- Ultimately victorious. You won the battle.

I have fought the good fight, I have finished the race, I have kept the faith (2 Timothy 4:7; NKJV).

- You are experiencing freedom from pain, losses, and rescued from affliction. AMEN.
- To come out stronger, we have to consider the following:

1. Our ways must please the Lord for Him to get on our side and rescue us.

What then shall we say to these things? If God is for us, who can be against us? (Romans 8:31; NKJV).

All the ways of a man are clean in his own eyes; but the Lord weigheth the spirits...When a man's ways please the Lord, he maketh even his enemies to be at peace with him (Proverbs 16:2, 7; NKJV).

2. You will always be preferred when God favours you. His favour shields you.

For You, O Lord, will bless the righteous; With favor You will surround him as with a shield (Psalm 5:12; NKJV).

3. New levels bring in new devils. Prepare and get ready for war. Be combatant ready.

Be sober, be vigilant; because your adversary the devil walks about like a roaring lion, seeking whom he may devour. Resist him, steadfast in the faith, knowing that the same sufferings are experienced by your brotherhood in the world (1 Peter 5:8-9; NKJV).

4. God's deliverance is always guaranteed in our affliction.

Many are the afflictions of the righteous, But the Lord delivers him out of them all (Psalm 34:19; NKJV).

5. Keep waxing greater, better, and stronger than your enemies. When you are better, you're better and not bitter. Envy is generated by the wicked.

He increased His people greatly, And made them stronger than their enemies (Psalm 105:24; NKJV).

6. When you love God and are unmoved by the fear of man, God lifts you up as you tread on lions under your feet.

Thou shalt tread upon the lion and adder: the young lion and the dragon shalt thou trample under feet. Because he hath set his love upon me, therefore will I deliver him: I will set him on high, because he hath known my name (Psalm 91:13-14; NKJV).

So we may boldly say: "The Lord is my helper; I will not fear. What can man do to me?" (Hebrews 13:6; NKJV).

7. Nothing shall by any means hurt us. Nothing can stand against the prayer of a righteous person. Therefore, you and I shall always need to PRAY.

Behold, I give you the authority to trample on serpents and scorpions, and over all the power of the enemy, and nothing shall by any means hurt you (Luke 10:19; NKJV).

HENCE, FOR US TO COME OUT STRONGER LIKE DANIEL, WE NEED TO SEEK GOD!!

When We Pray

1. God fights for us.

The Lord will fight for you, and you shall hold your peace" (Exodus 14:14; NKJV).

2. We Influence other people around us to pray.

As iron sharpens iron, So a man sharpens the countenance of his friend (Proverbs 27:17; NKJV).

3. The value of the anointing and power for signs and wonders increases.

Two are better than one, Because they have a good reward for their labor (Ecclesiastes 4:9; NKJV).

4. Angels are sent into operation to assist us.

For He shall give His angels charge over you, To keep you in all your ways (Psalm 91:11; NKJV).

And of the angels He says: "Who makes His angels spirits And His ministers a flame of fire." … Are they not all ministering spirits sent forth to minister for those who will inherit salvation? (Hebrews 1:7 & 14).

5. Our desires are granted, and expectations are met.

You open Your hand And satisfy the desire of every living thing (Psalm 145:16; NKJV).

6. We experience long-term deliverance from long-term issues and problems.

I waited patiently for the Lord; And He inclined to me, And heard my cry. He also brought me up out of a horrible pit, Out of the miry clay, And set my feet upon a rock, And established my steps. He has put a new song in my mouth—Praise to our God; Many will see it and fear, And will trust in the Lord (Psalm 40:1-3).

7. Those who God will use for us won't be at peace and won't be able to sleep till they arise to help us.

You hold my eyelids open; I am so troubled that I cannot speak (Psalm 77:4; NKJV).

That night the king could not sleep. So one was commanded to bring the book of the records of the chronicles; and they were read before the king (Esther 6:1; NKJV).

Now the king went to his palace and spent the night fasting; and no musicians were brought before him. Also his sleep went from him (Daniel 6:18; NKJV).

8. Illegal laws and evil decrees are changed for the best.

I make a decree that in every dominion of my kingdom men must tremble and fear before the God of Daniel. For He is the living God, And steadfast forever; His kingdom is the one which shall not be destroyed, And His dominion shall endure to the end (Daniel 6:26; NKJV).

9. Outbreak of revival.

O Lord, I have heard Your speech and was afraid; O Lord, revive Your work in the midst of the years! In the midst of the years make it known; In wrath remember mercy (Habakkuk 3:2; NKJV).

Then those who gladly received his word were baptized; and that day about three thousand souls were added to them (Acts 2:41; NKJV).

However, many of those who heard the word believed; and the number of the men came to be about five thousand (Acts 4:4; NKJV).

DECLARATIONS

For someone locked up in the den or life or cave, come out!

You've been too long in the hole... be pulled out.

Your seat of honour, favour, victory, and celebration shall not be empty.

Come out of the den of shame, embarrassment, unfruitfulness, sorrow, debt, slavery, and bondage.

Anyone tied up in the hole or den must be released into your calling, destiny, purpose, ministry, favour, and prosperity.

REFERENCES

i) Excerpts from the teaching ministry of Rev George Adegboye. {Ever Increasing Word Ministries & George Adegboye World Outreach}.

ii) Innovations from Felix Makanjuola, Jnr.